The Big Sky

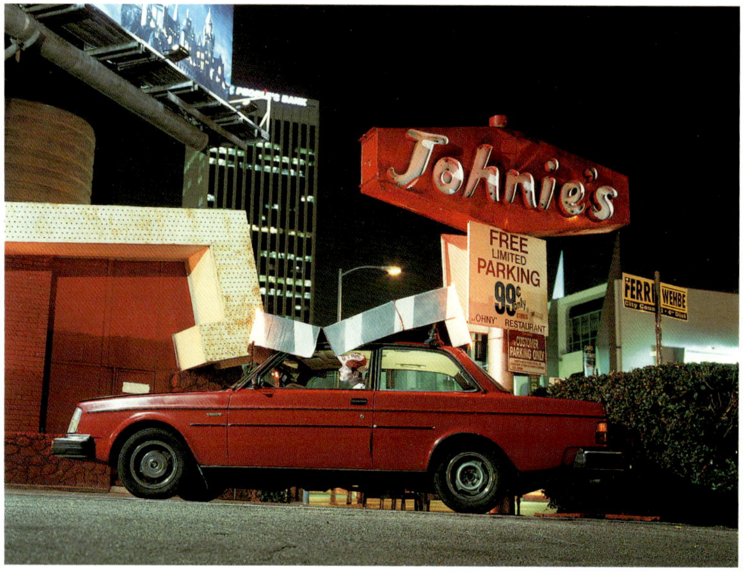
Johnie's
FREE
LIMITED
PARKING
99¢ only
"OHNY" RESTAURANT
CUSTOMER PARKING ONLY
FERRI
WEHBE

Eva Castringius

The Big Sky

Los Angeles—Berlin

jovis

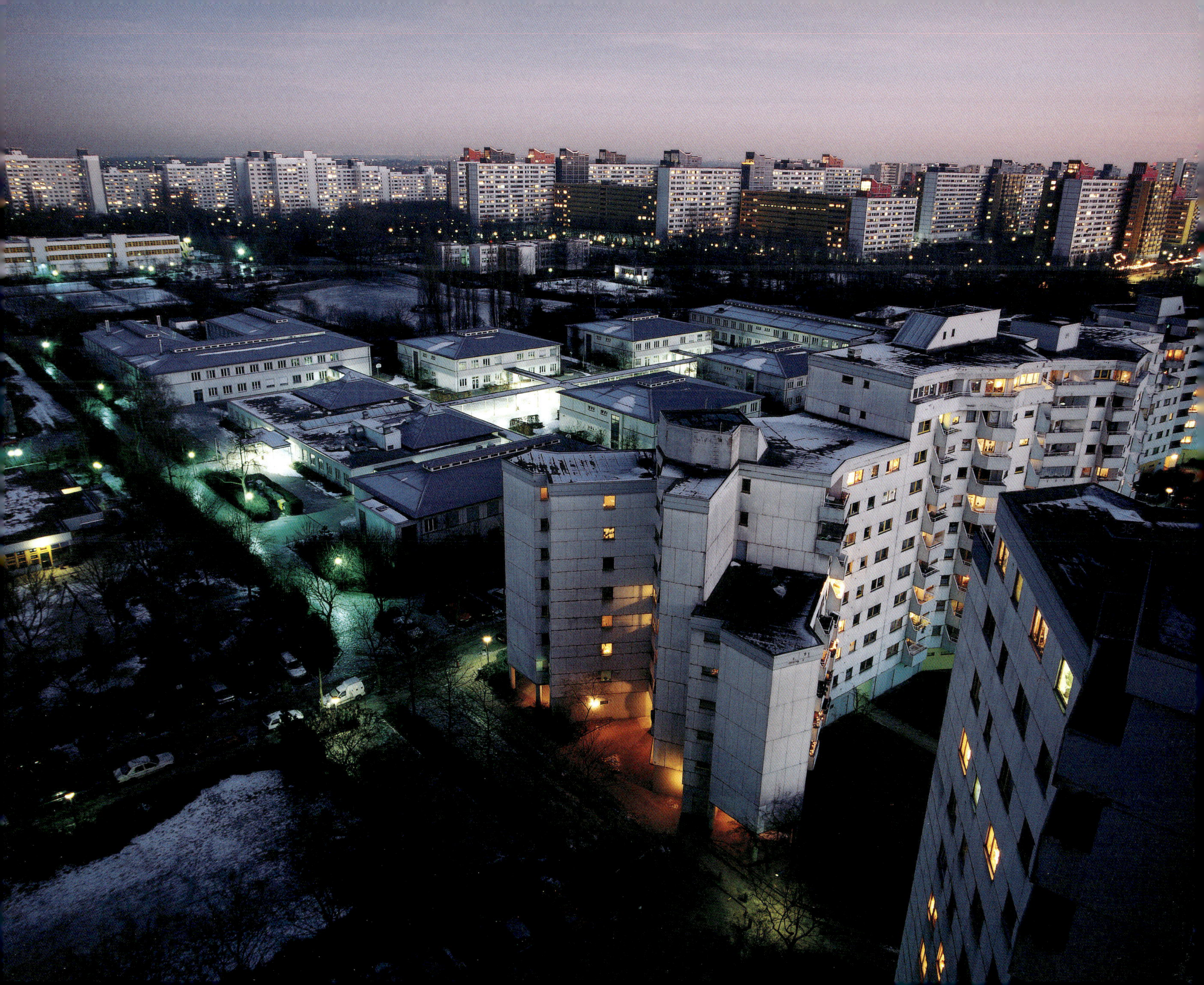

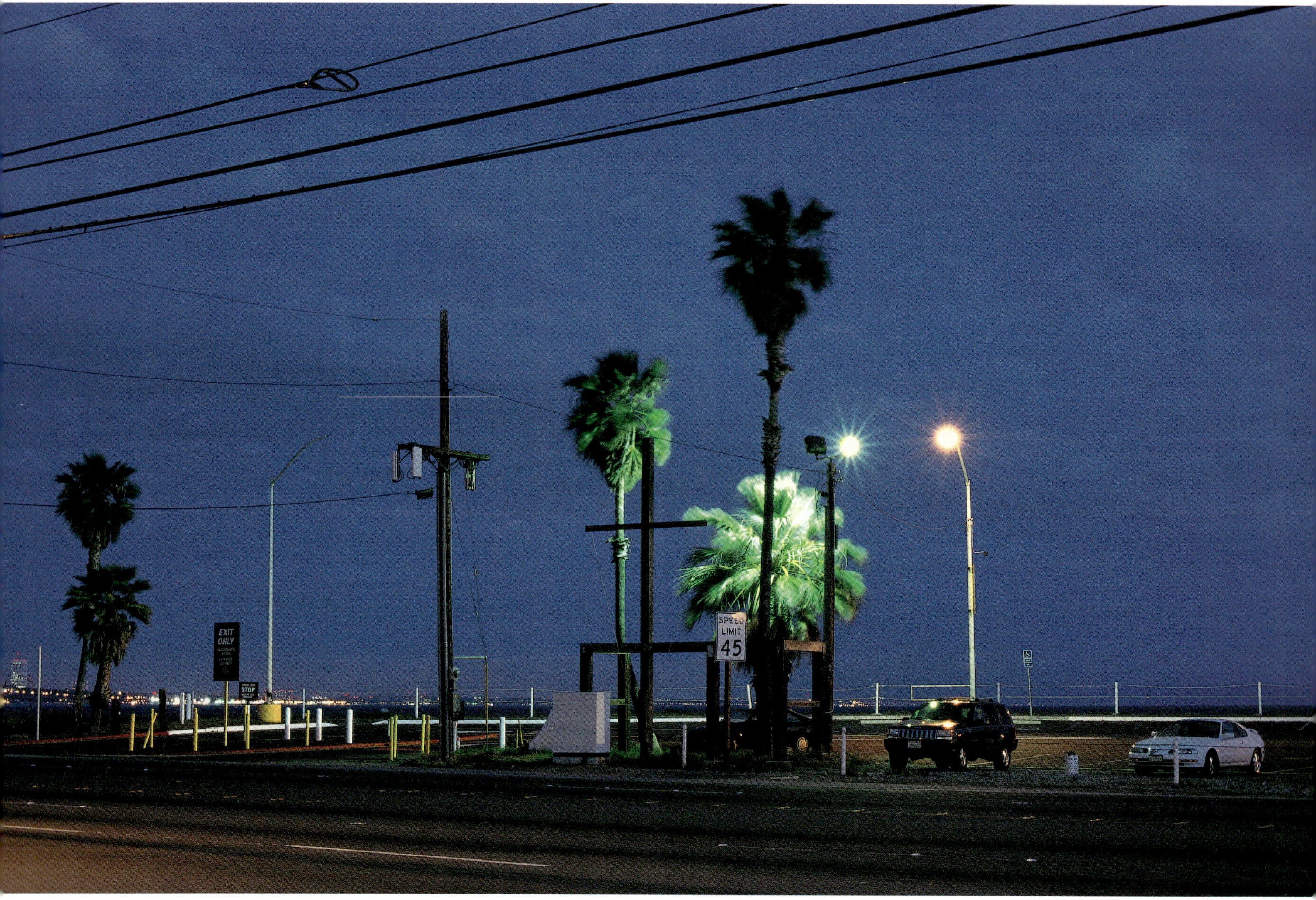
EXIT ONLY
STOP
SPEED LIMIT 45

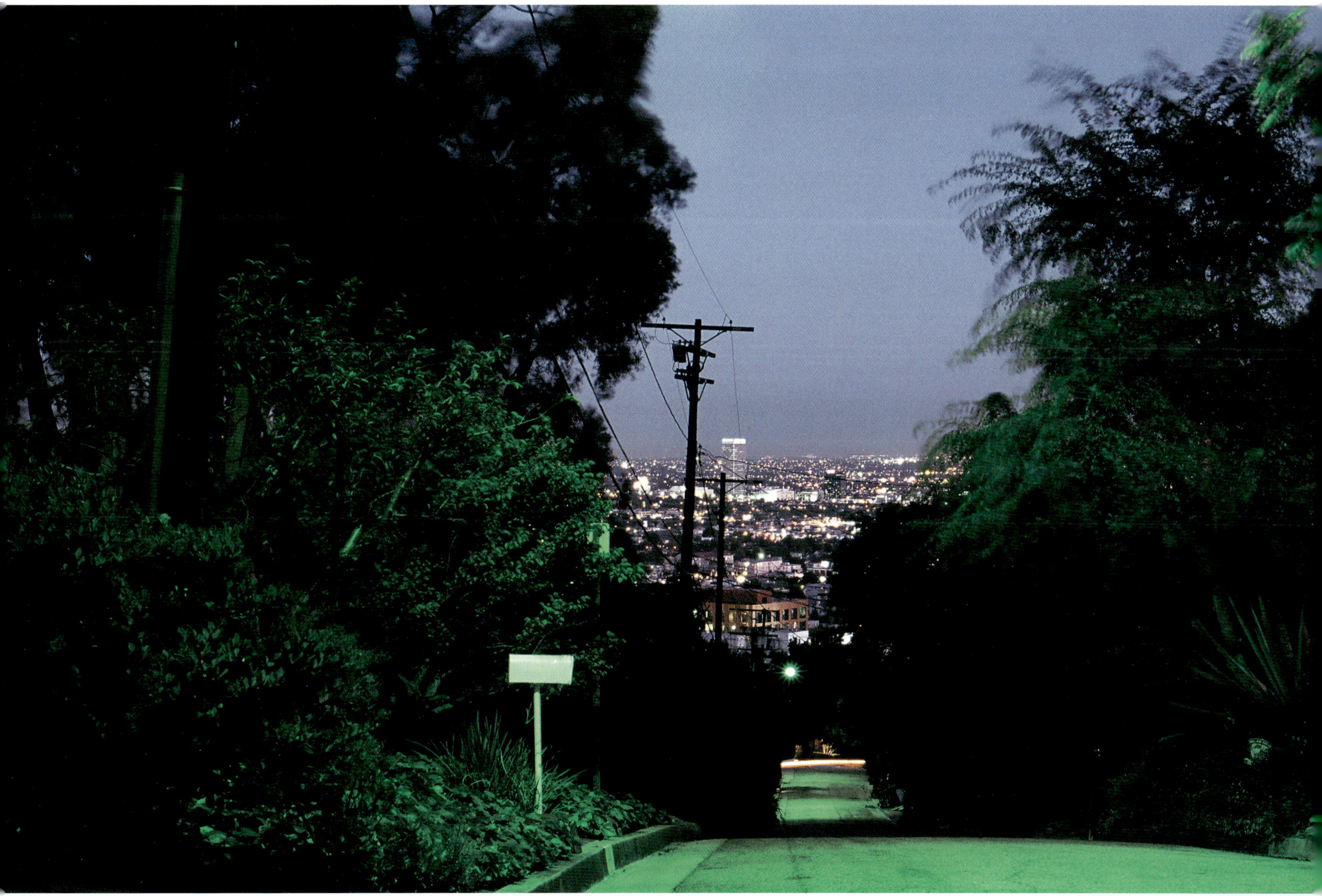

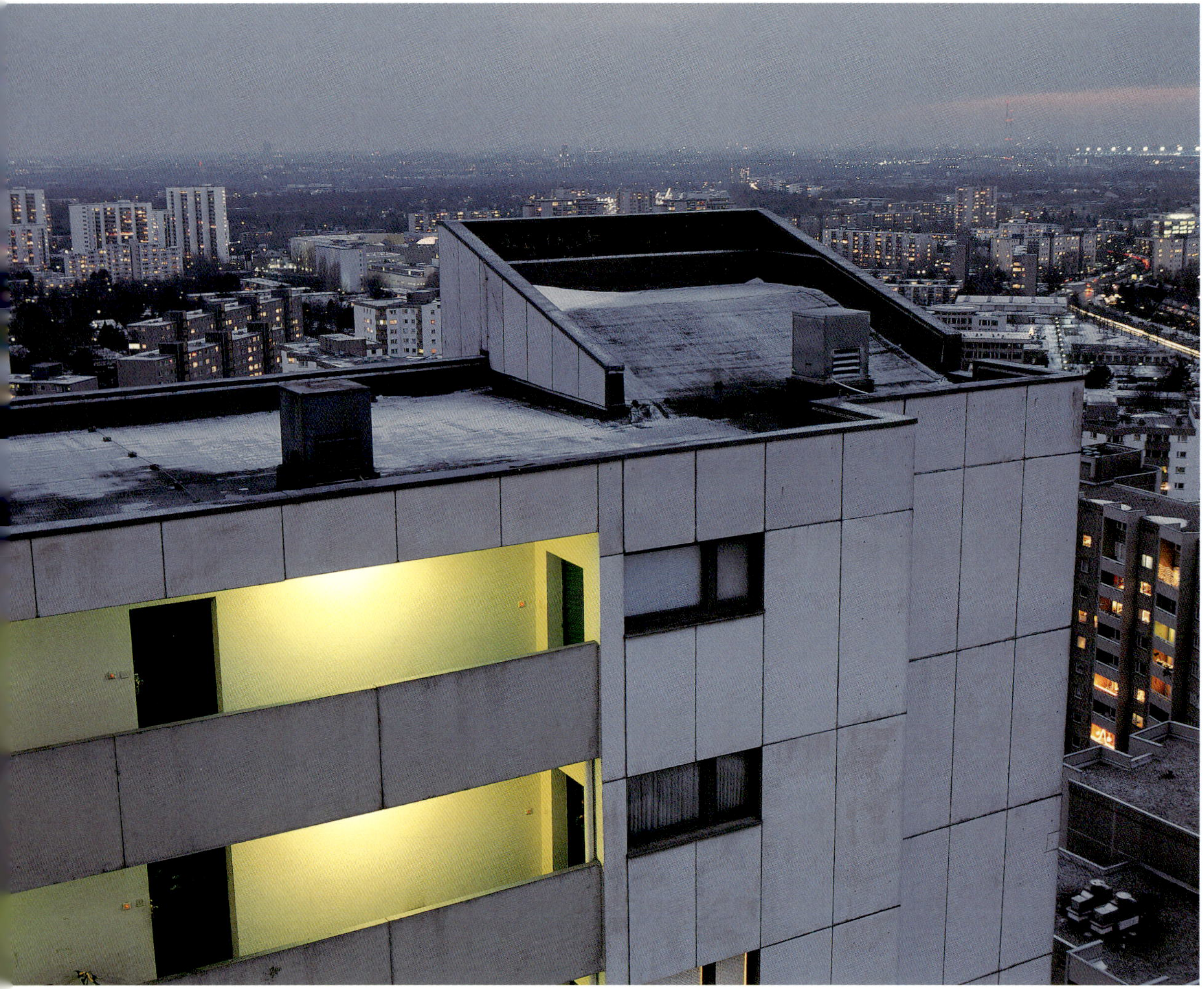

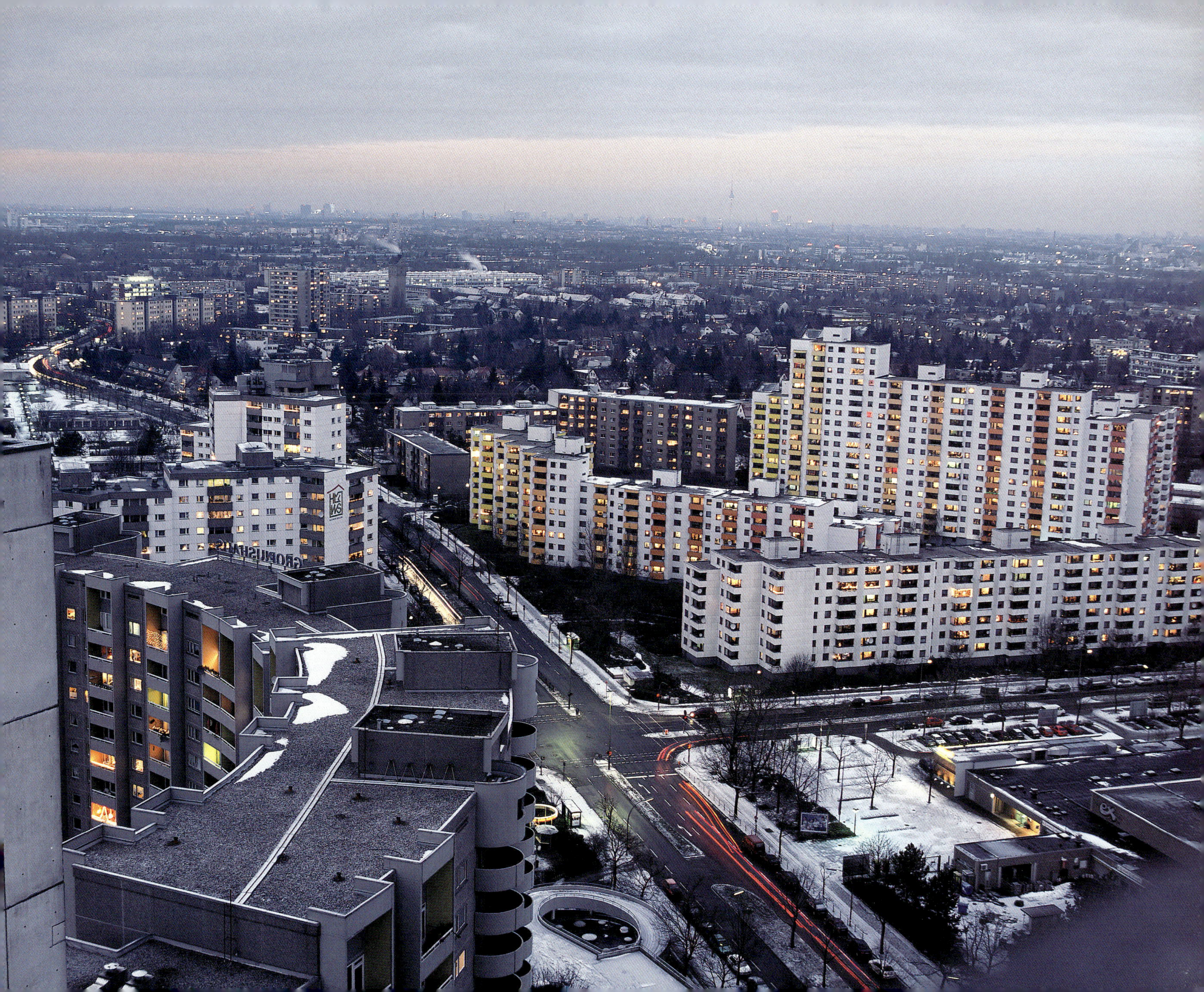

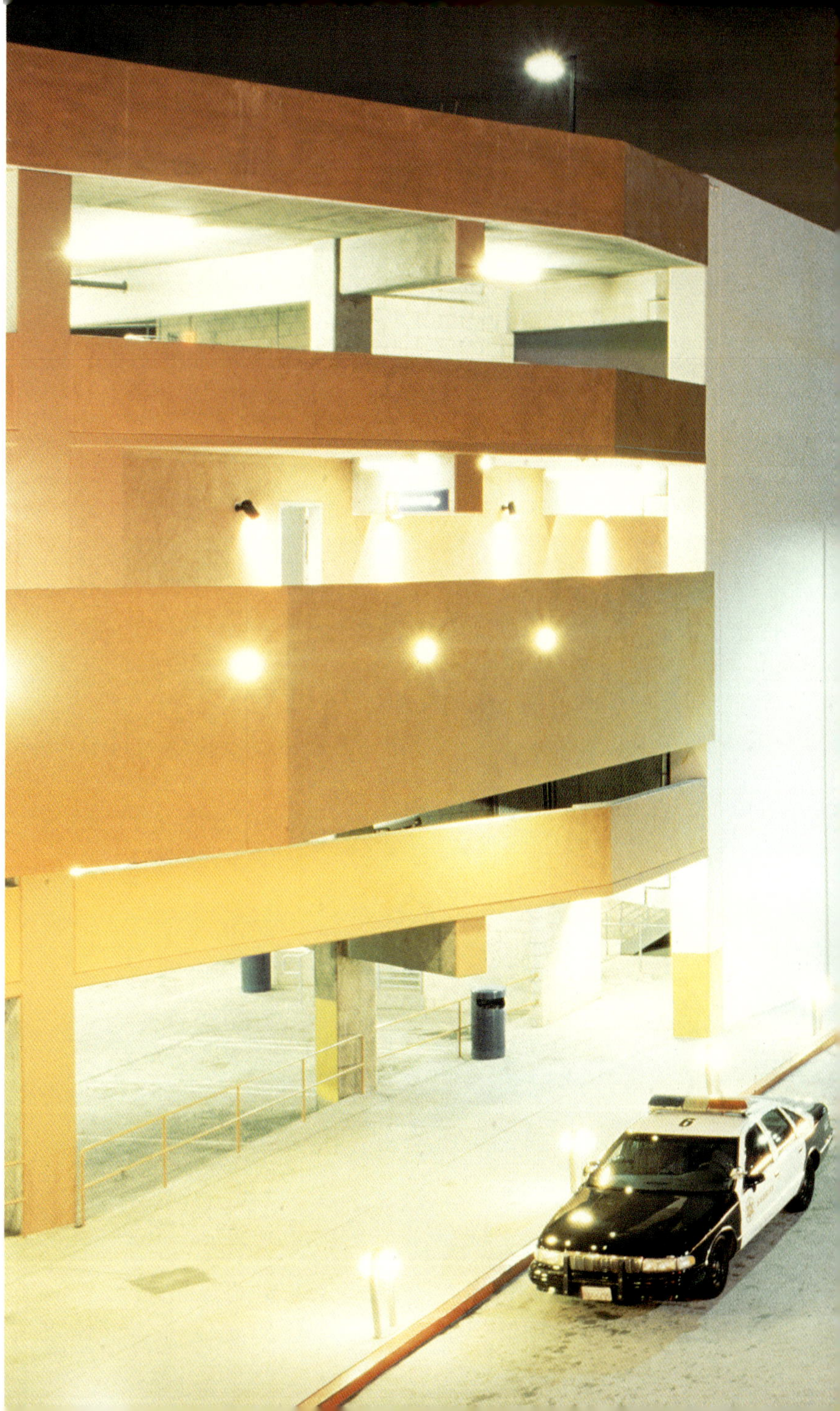

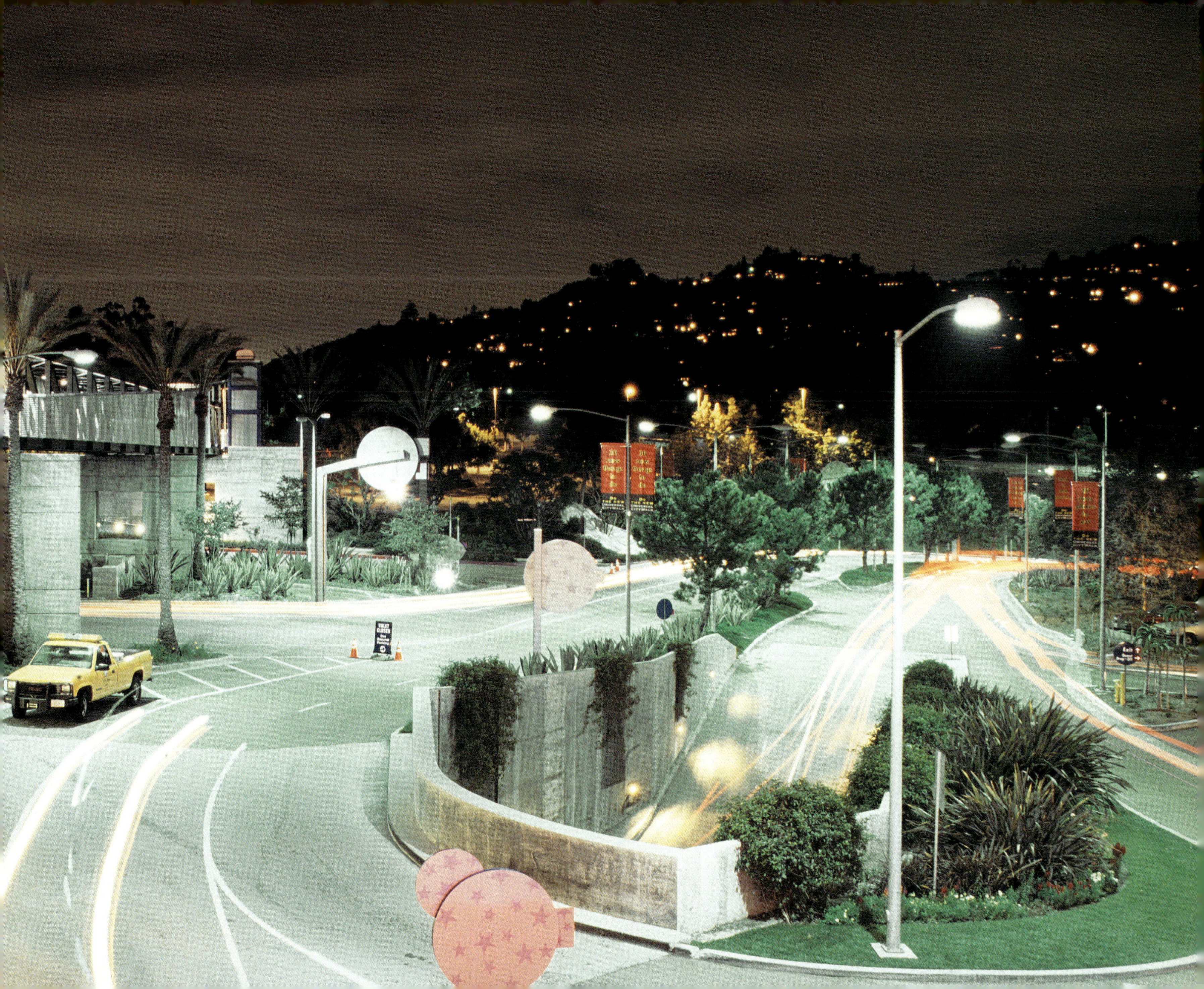

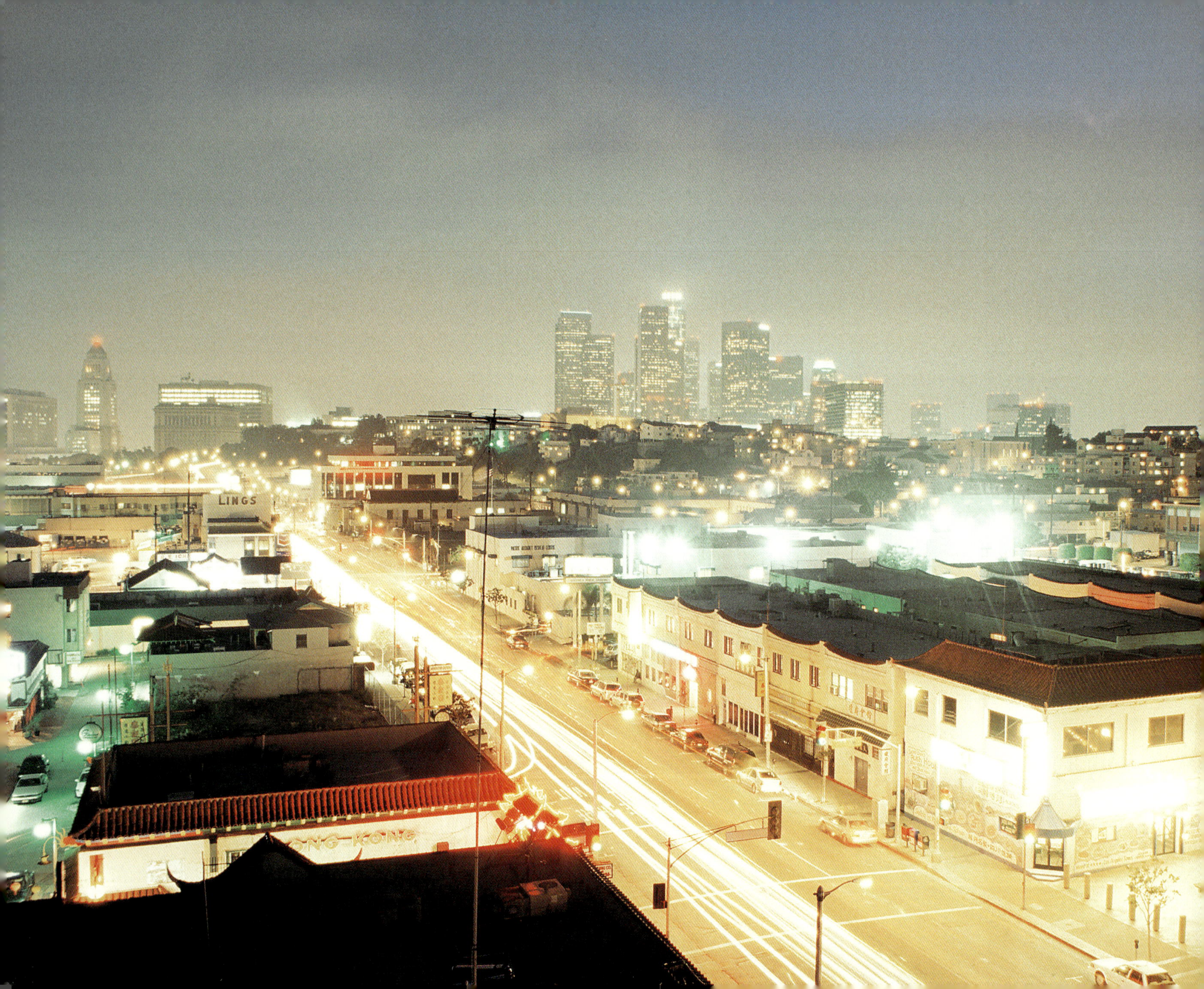
LINGS

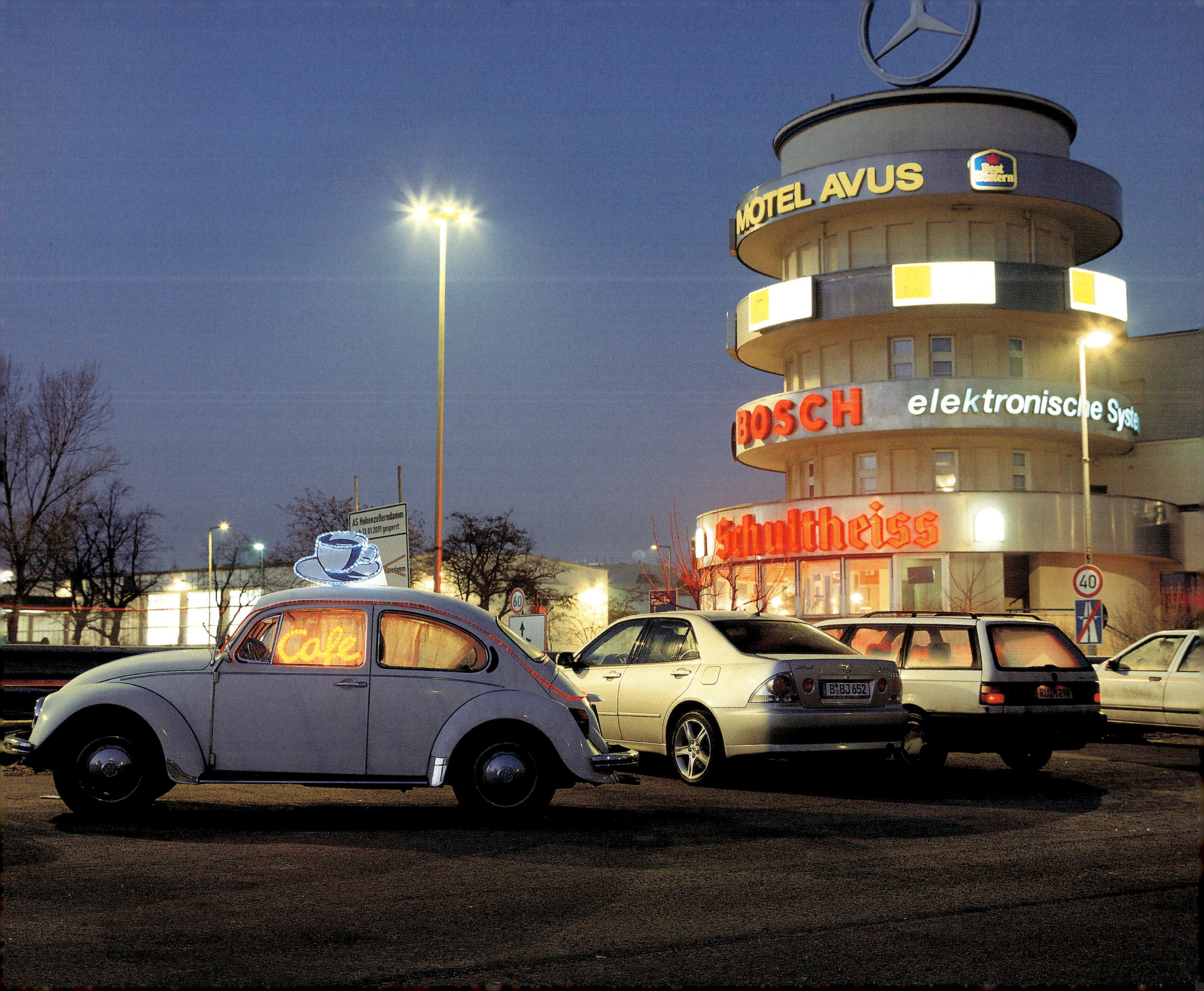
MOTEL AVUS
BOSCH
elektronische
Schultheiss
Cafe
40
60

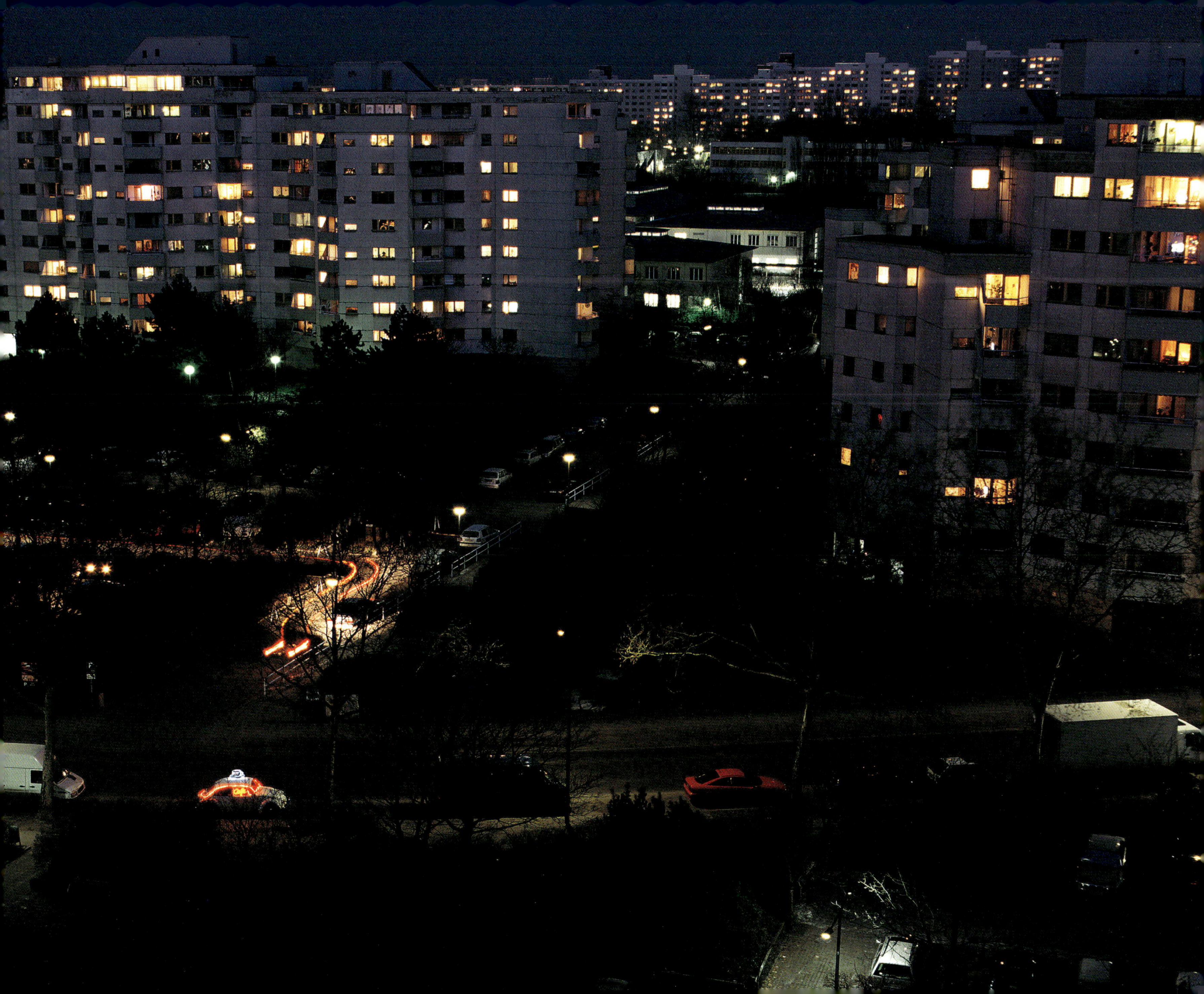

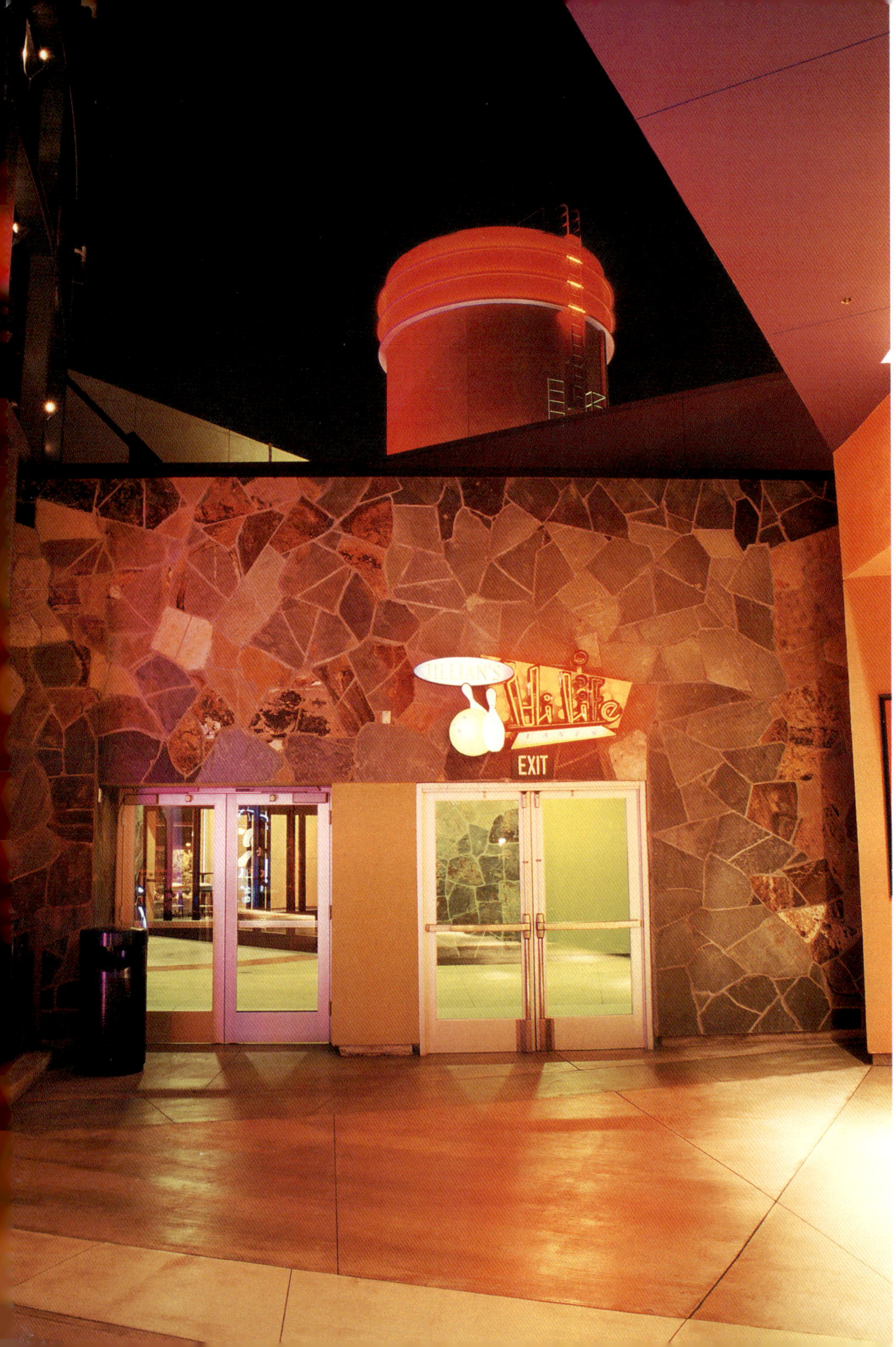
JILLIAN'S
Hi Life
LANES
EXIT

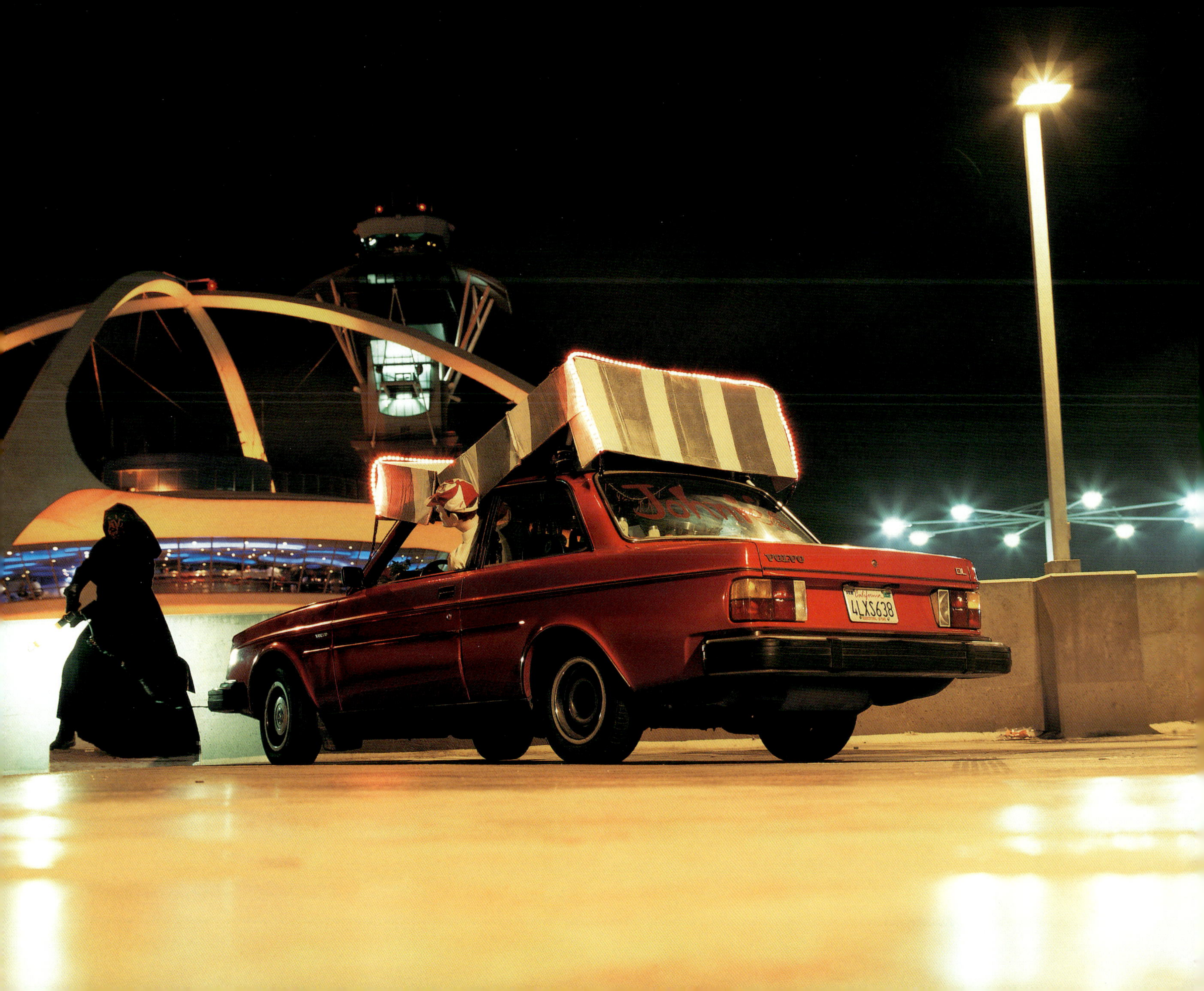
VOLVO
California
4LXS638

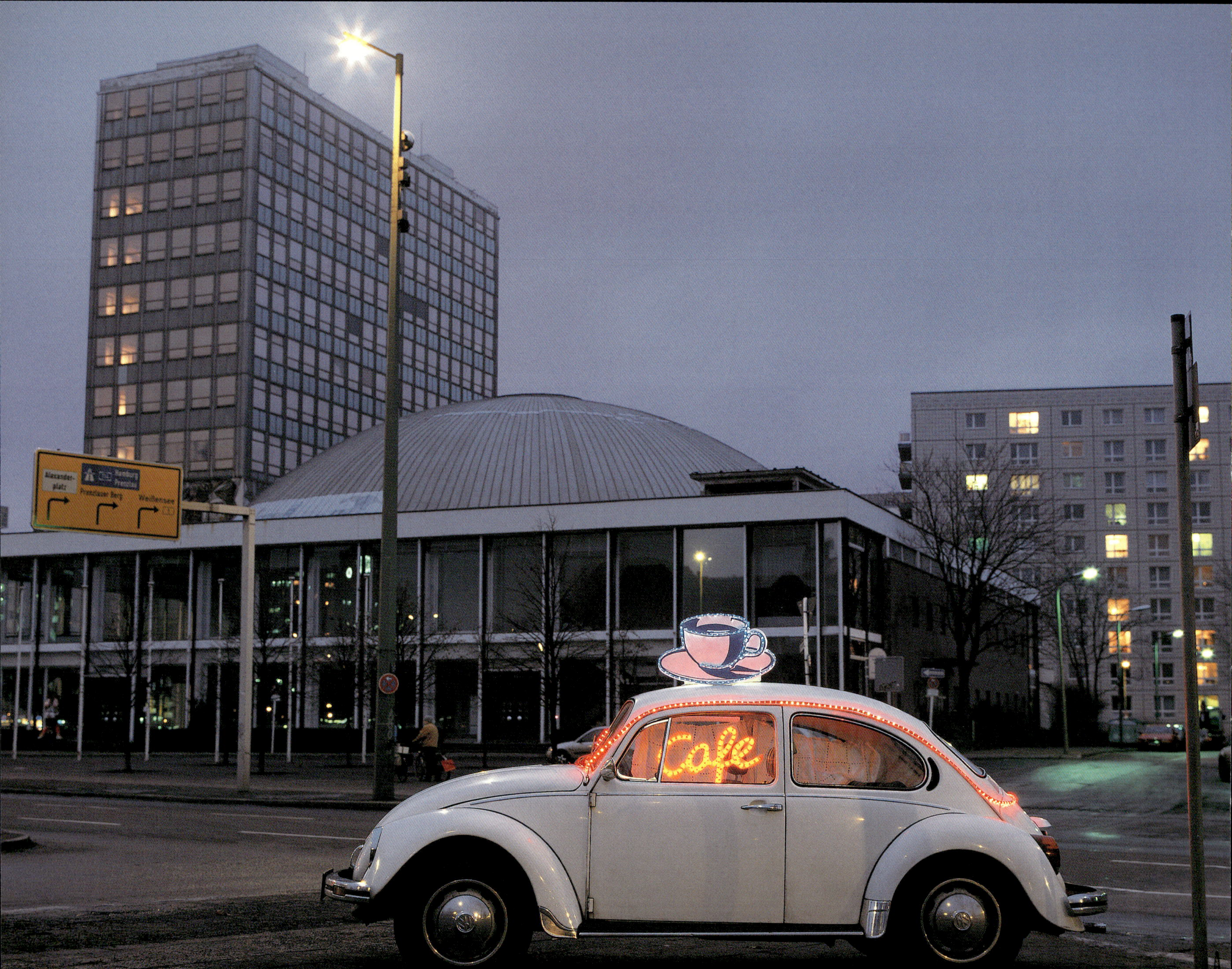
Cafe

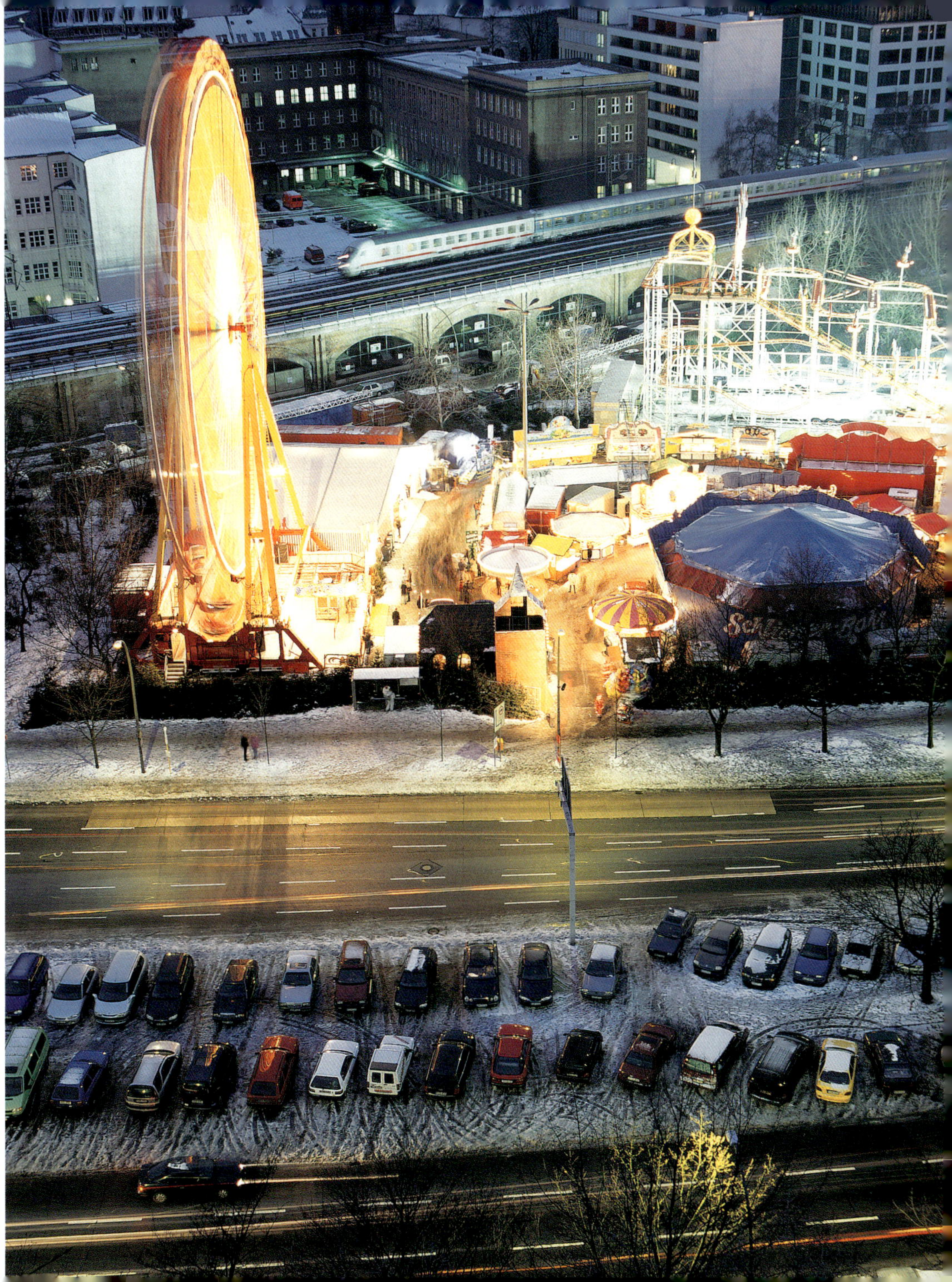

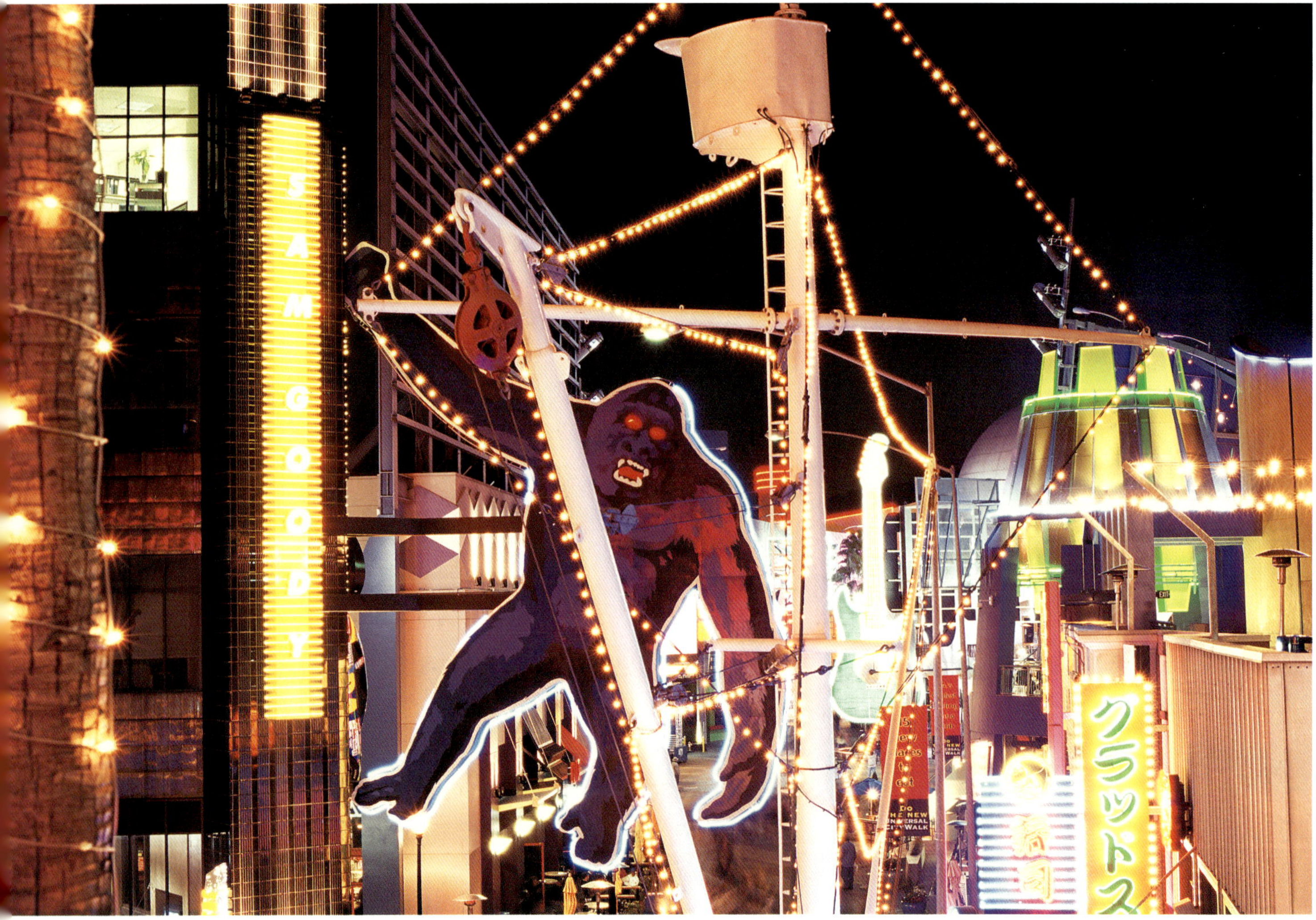
SAM GOODY
クラット

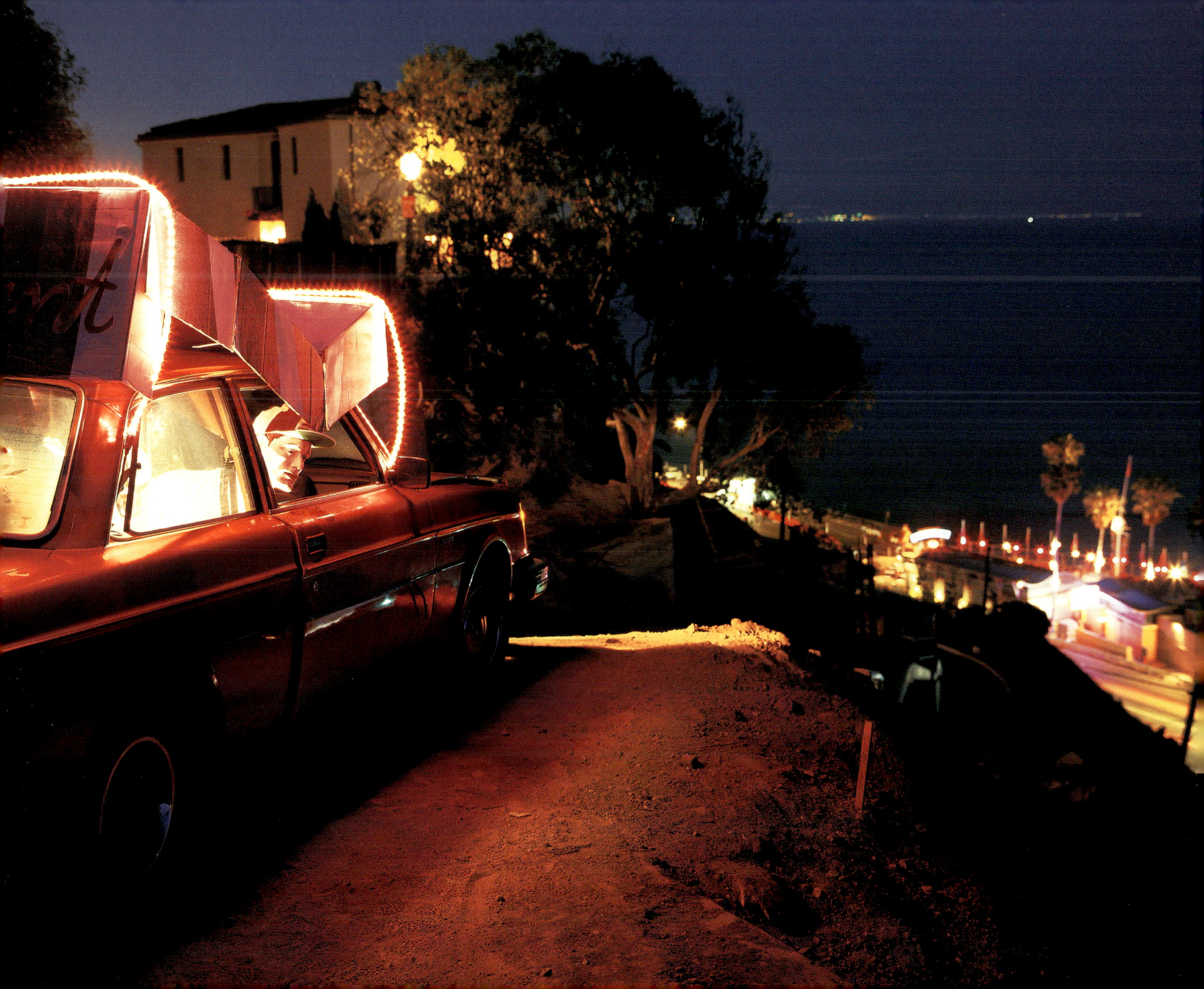

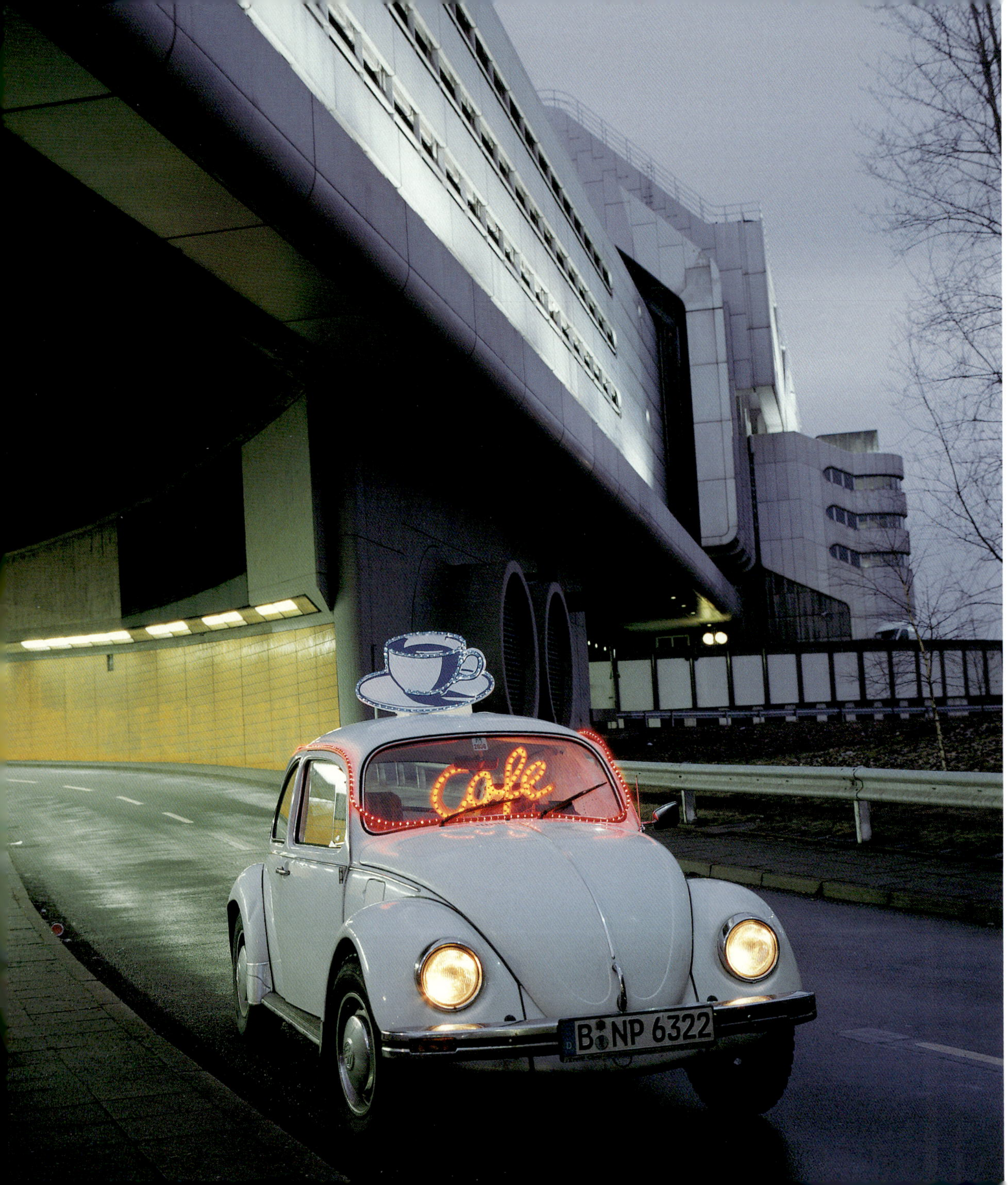
Cafe
B NP 6322

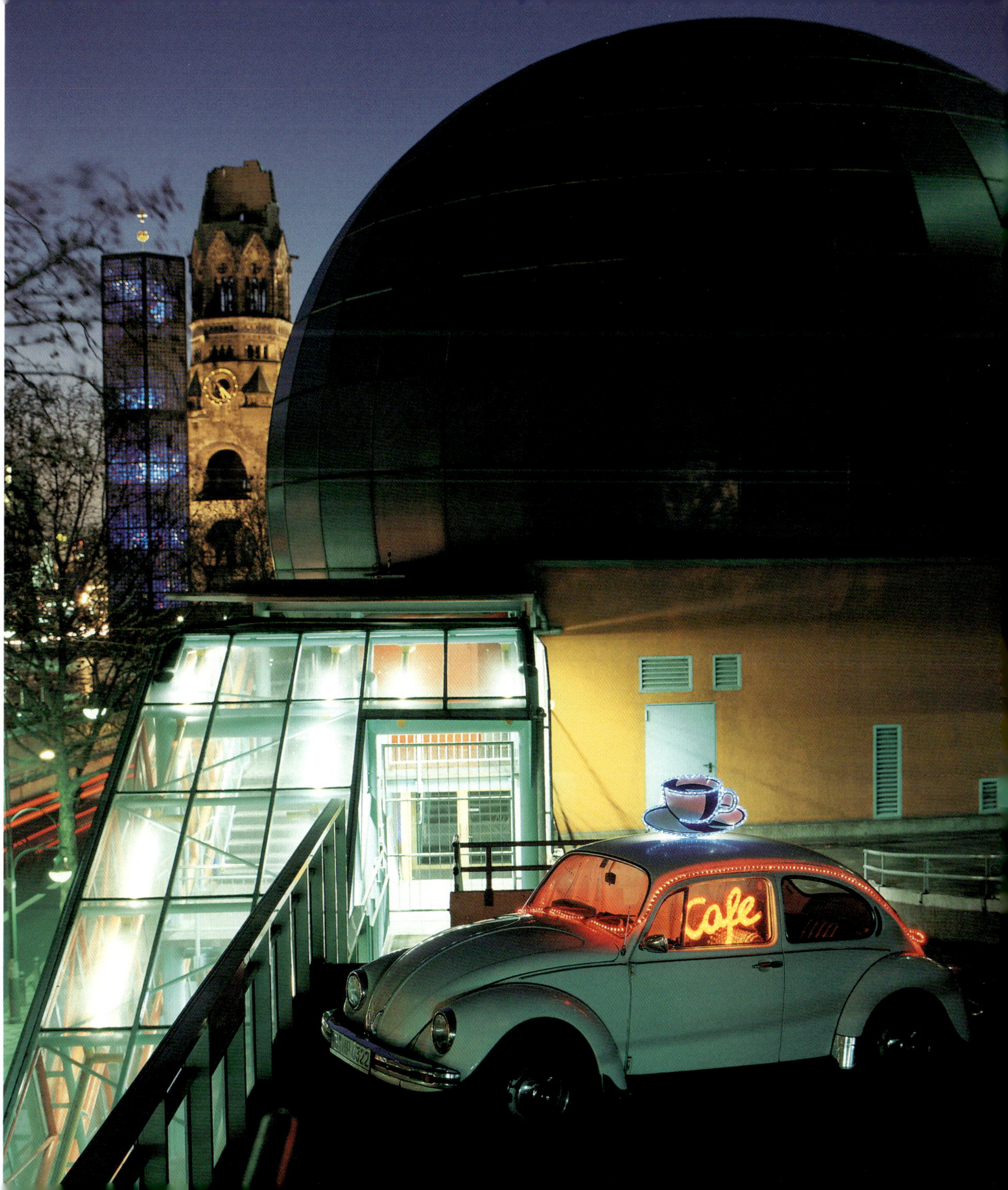
Cafe

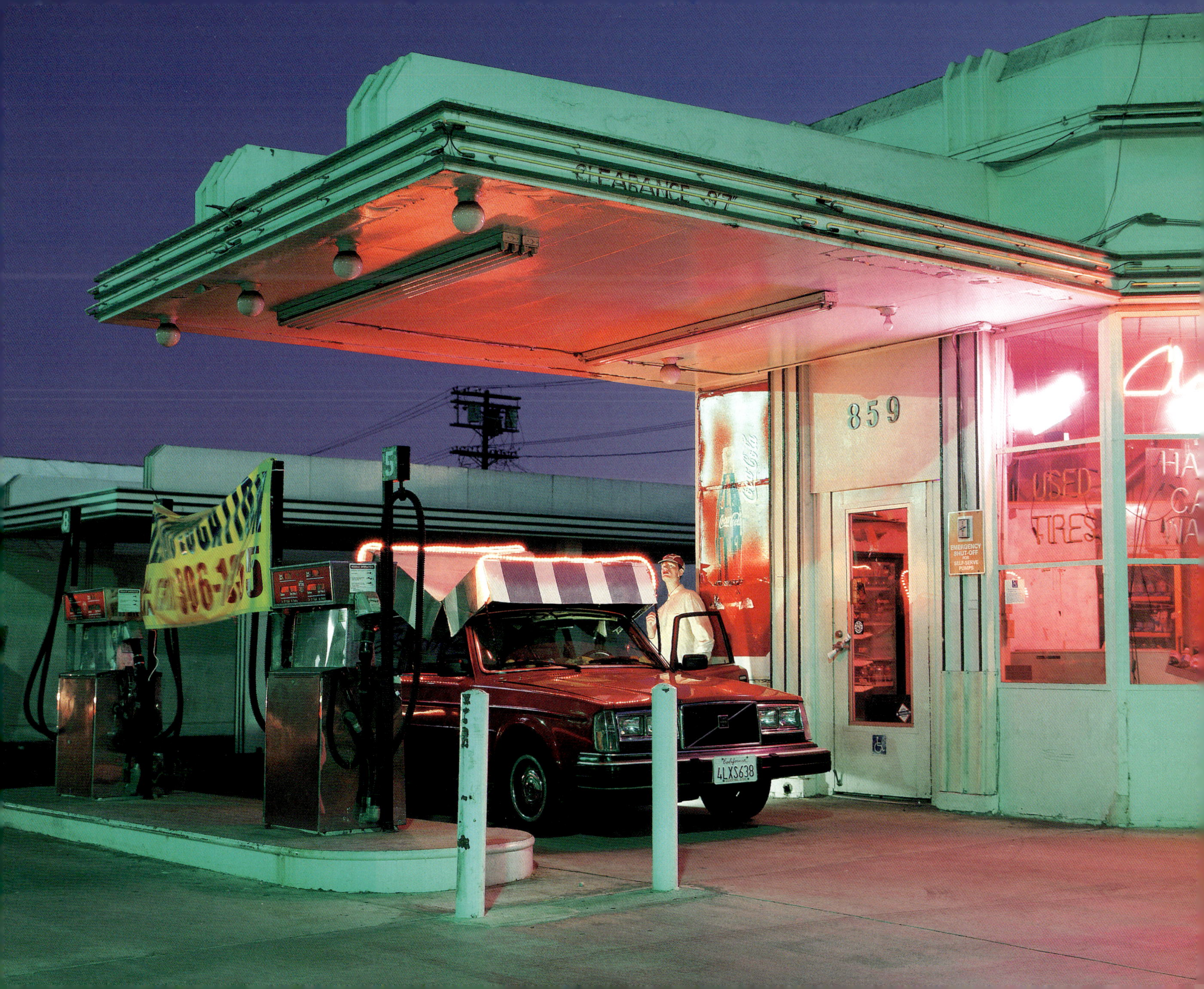
859
USED TIRES
EMERGENCY SHUT-OFF FOR SELF-SERVE PUMPS
4LXS638

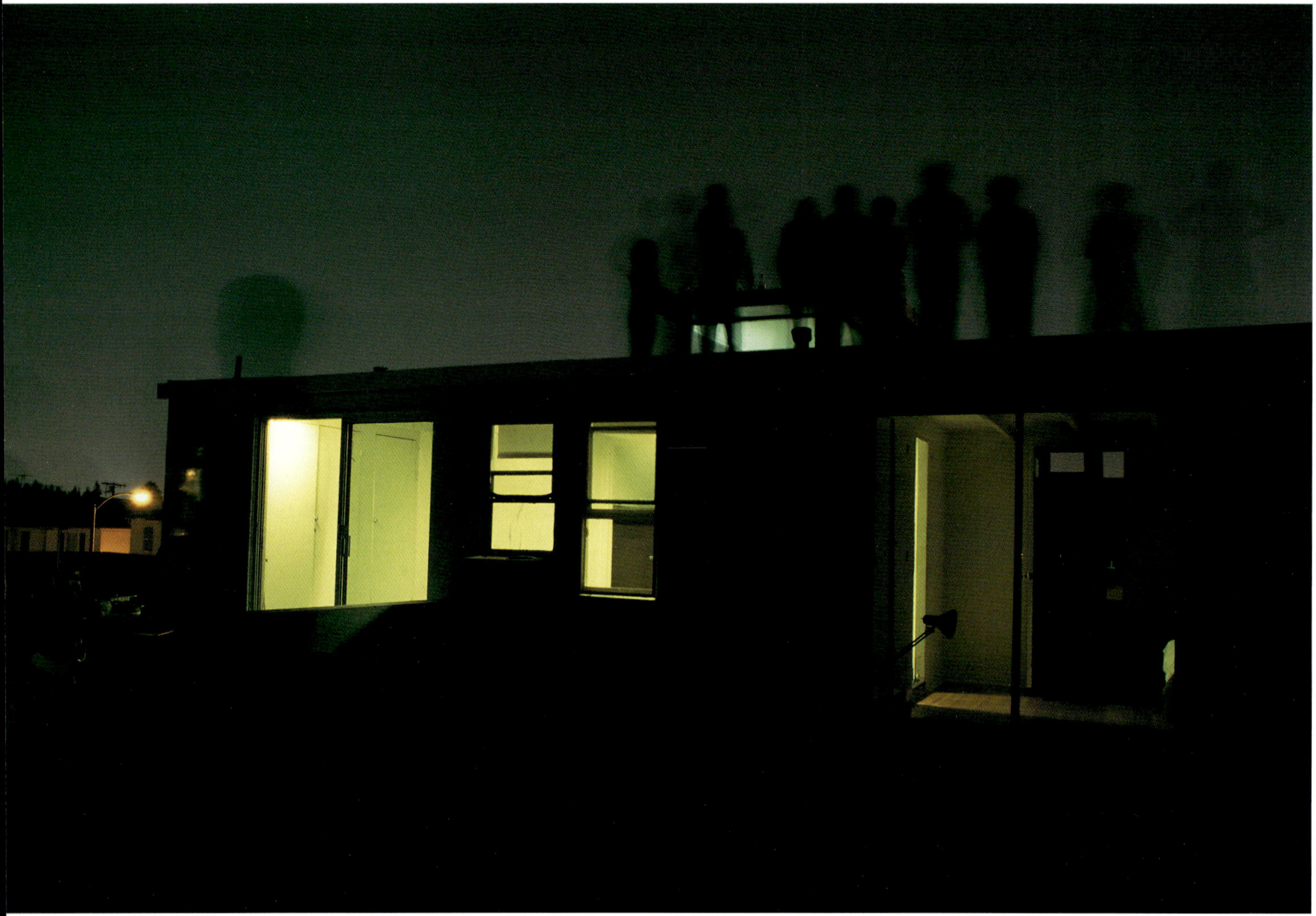

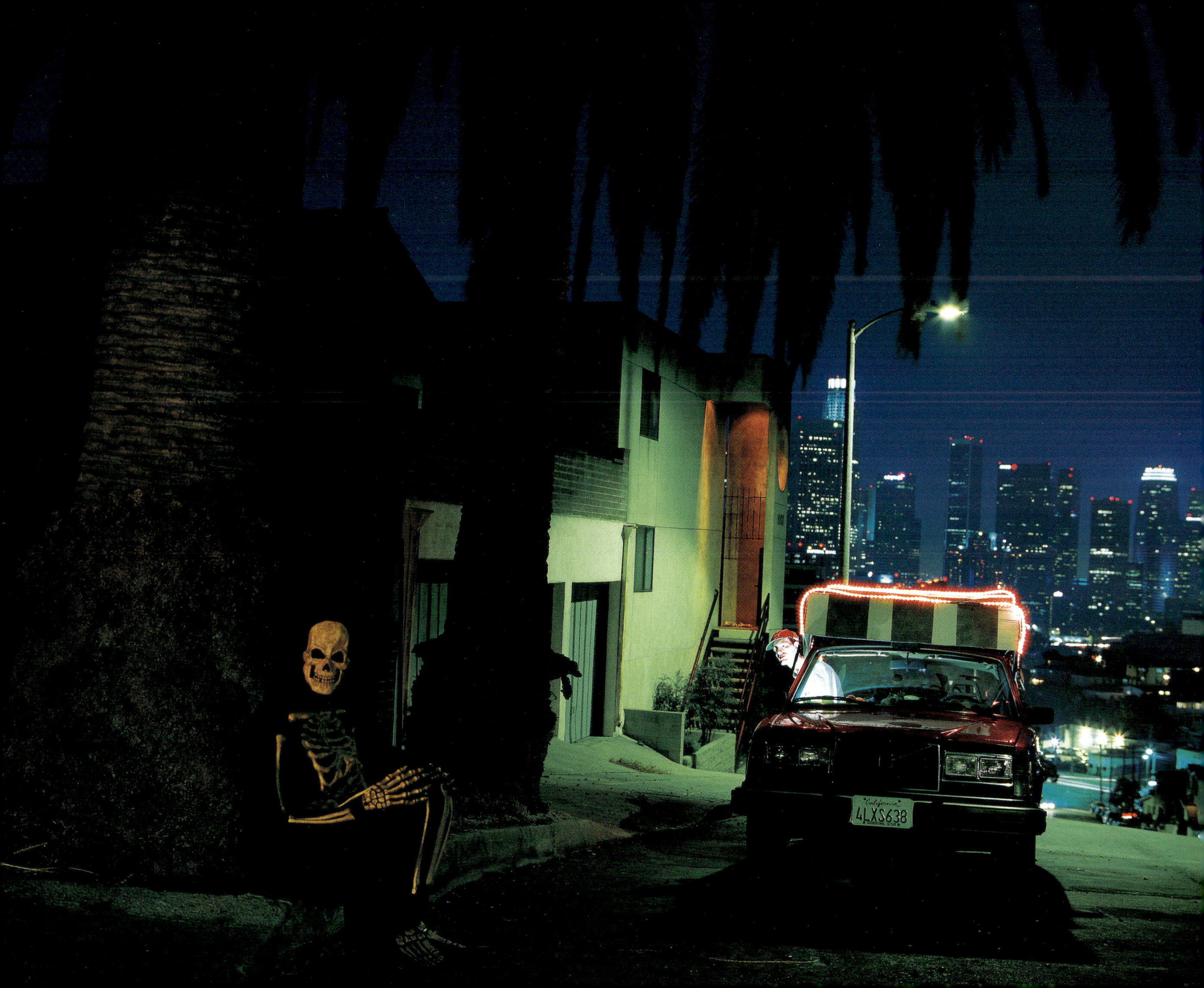
California
4LXS638

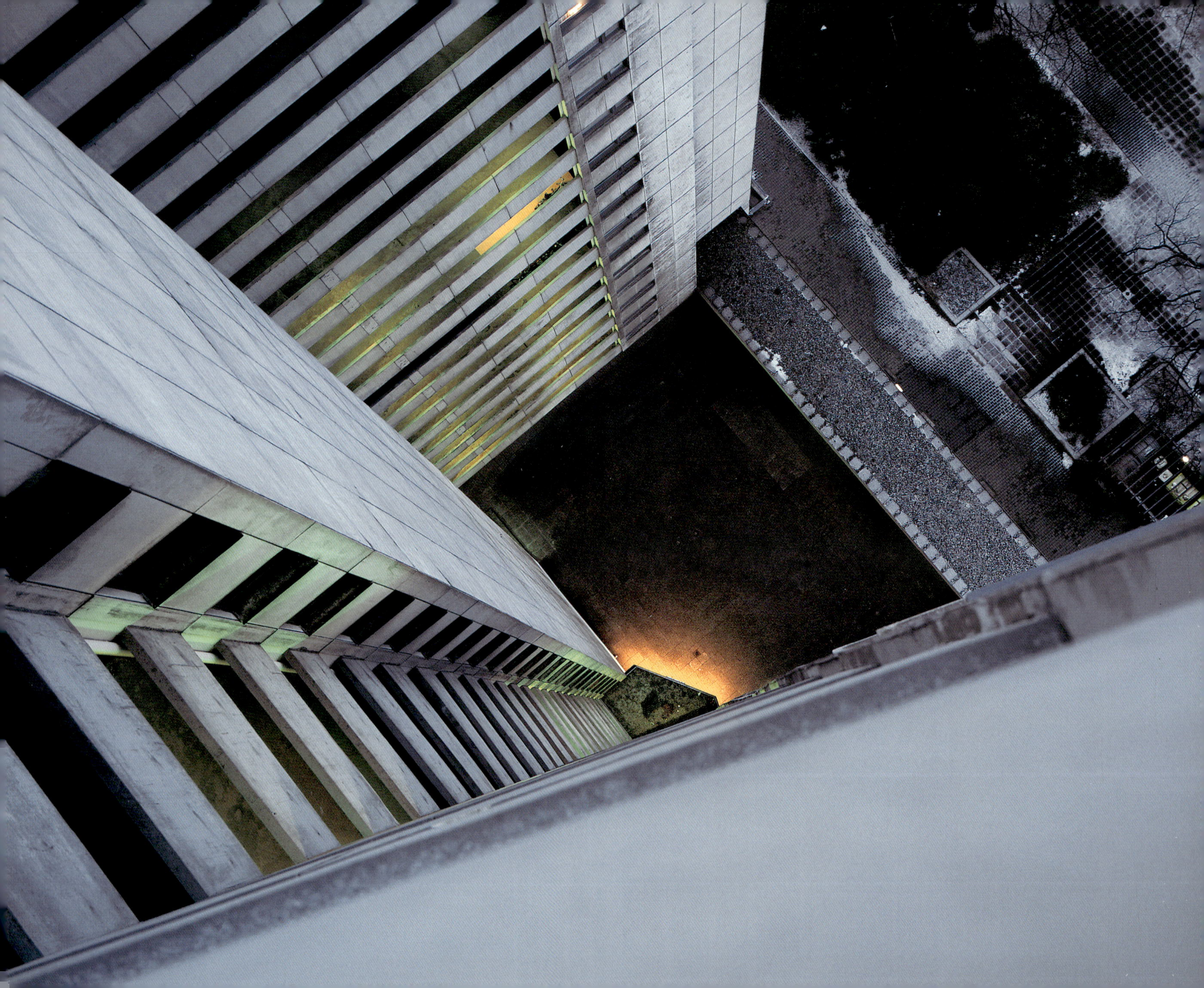

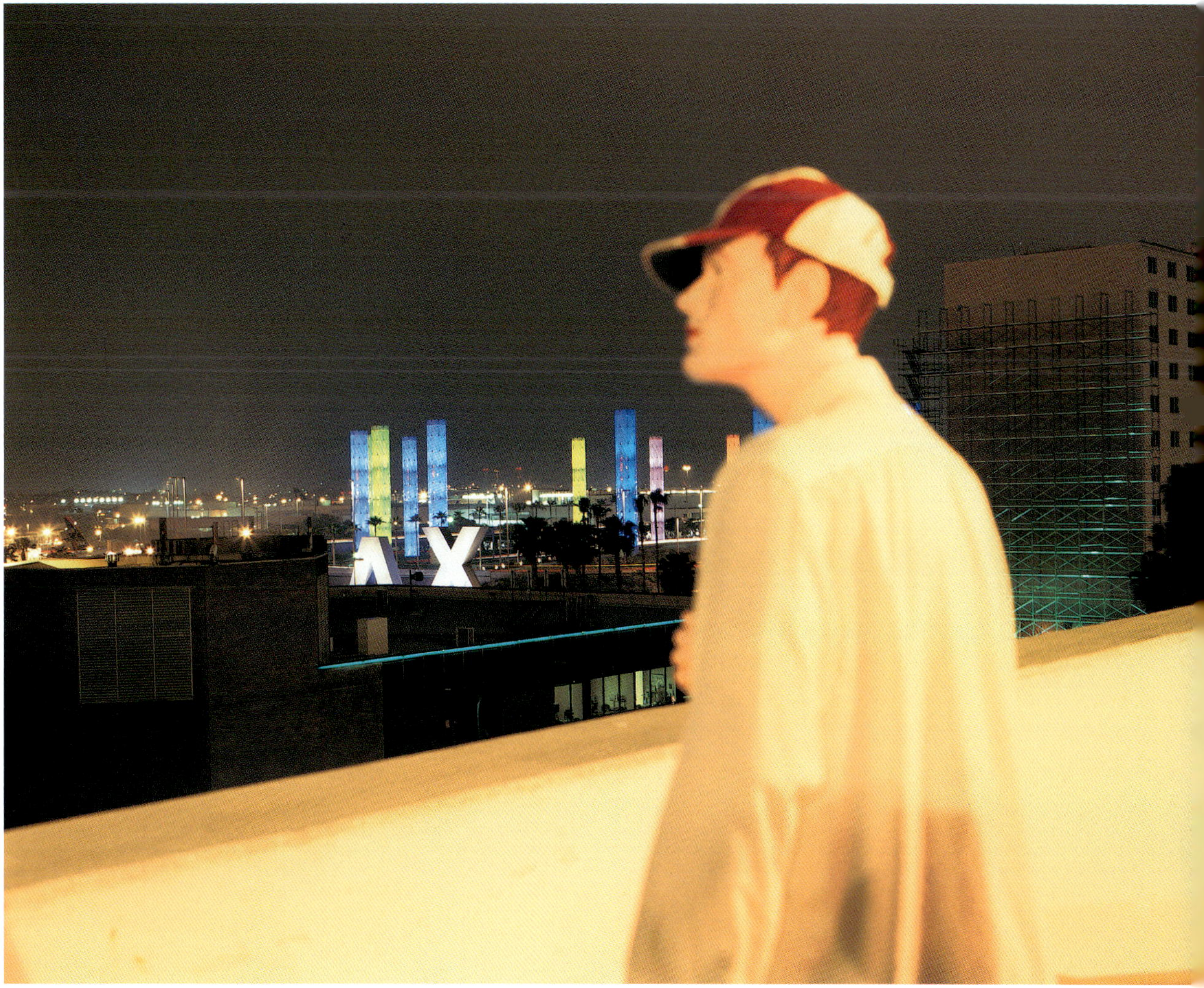
AX

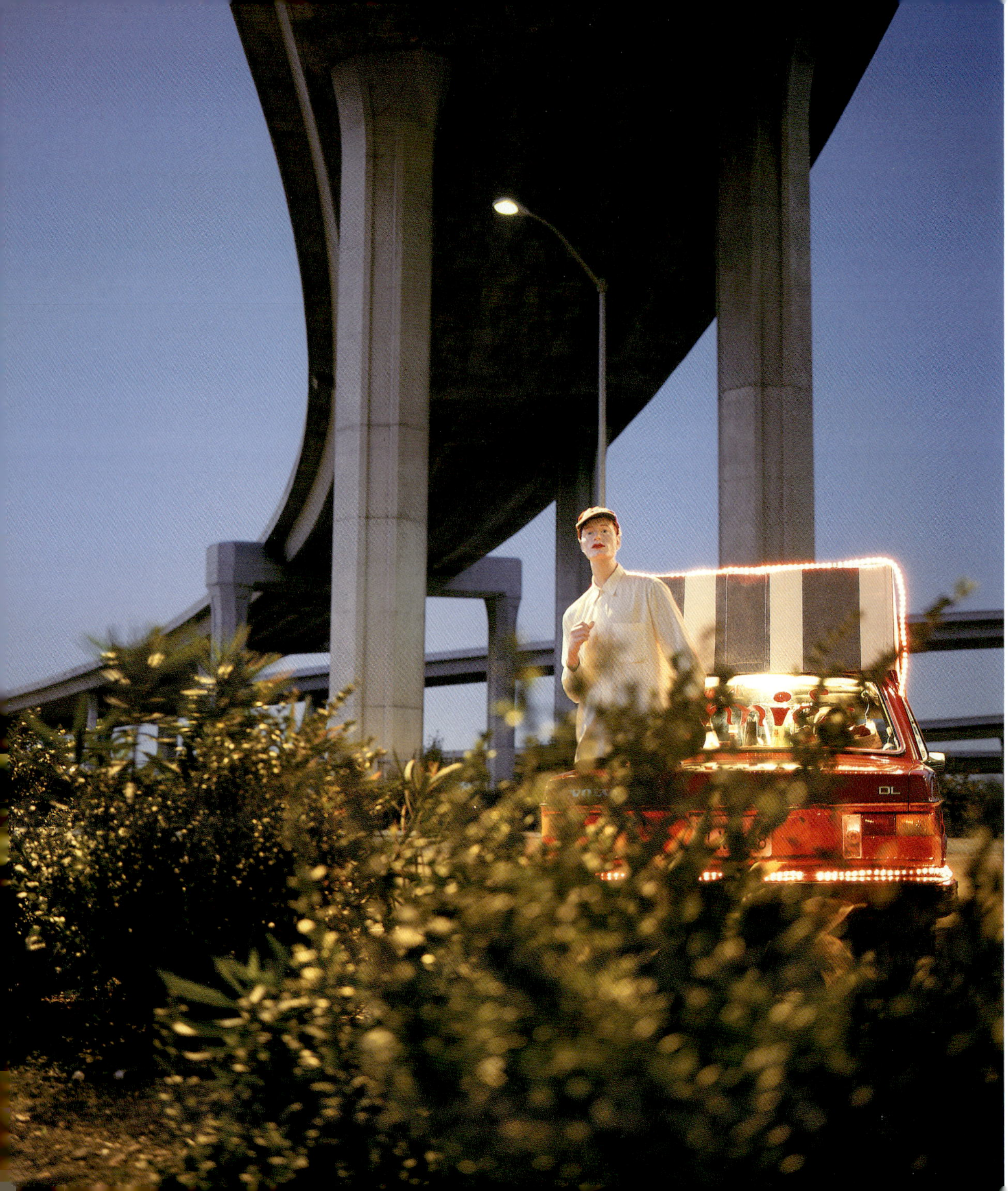
DL

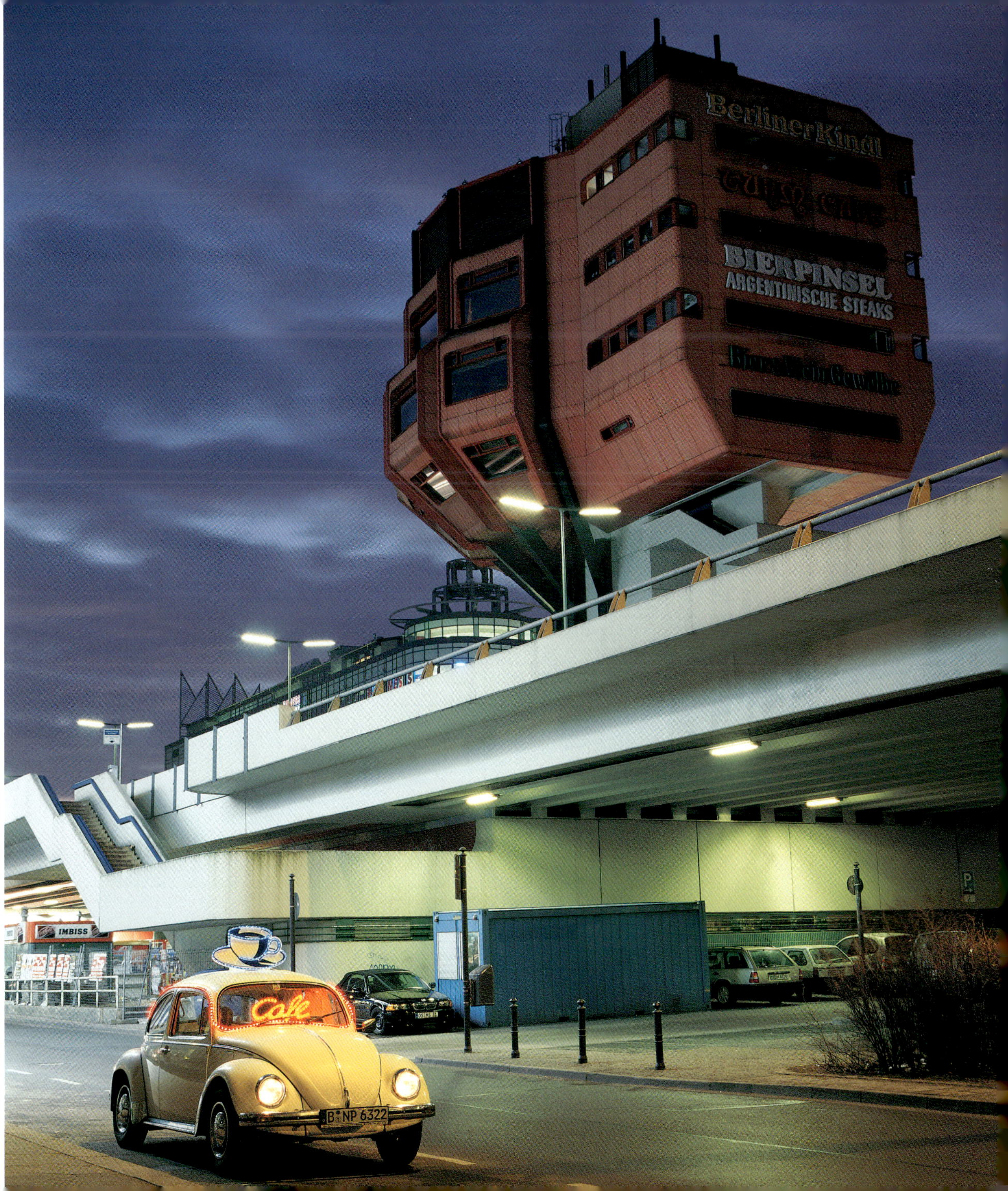
BerlinerKindl
BIERPINSEL
ARGENTINISCHE STEAKS
IMBISS
B NP 6322

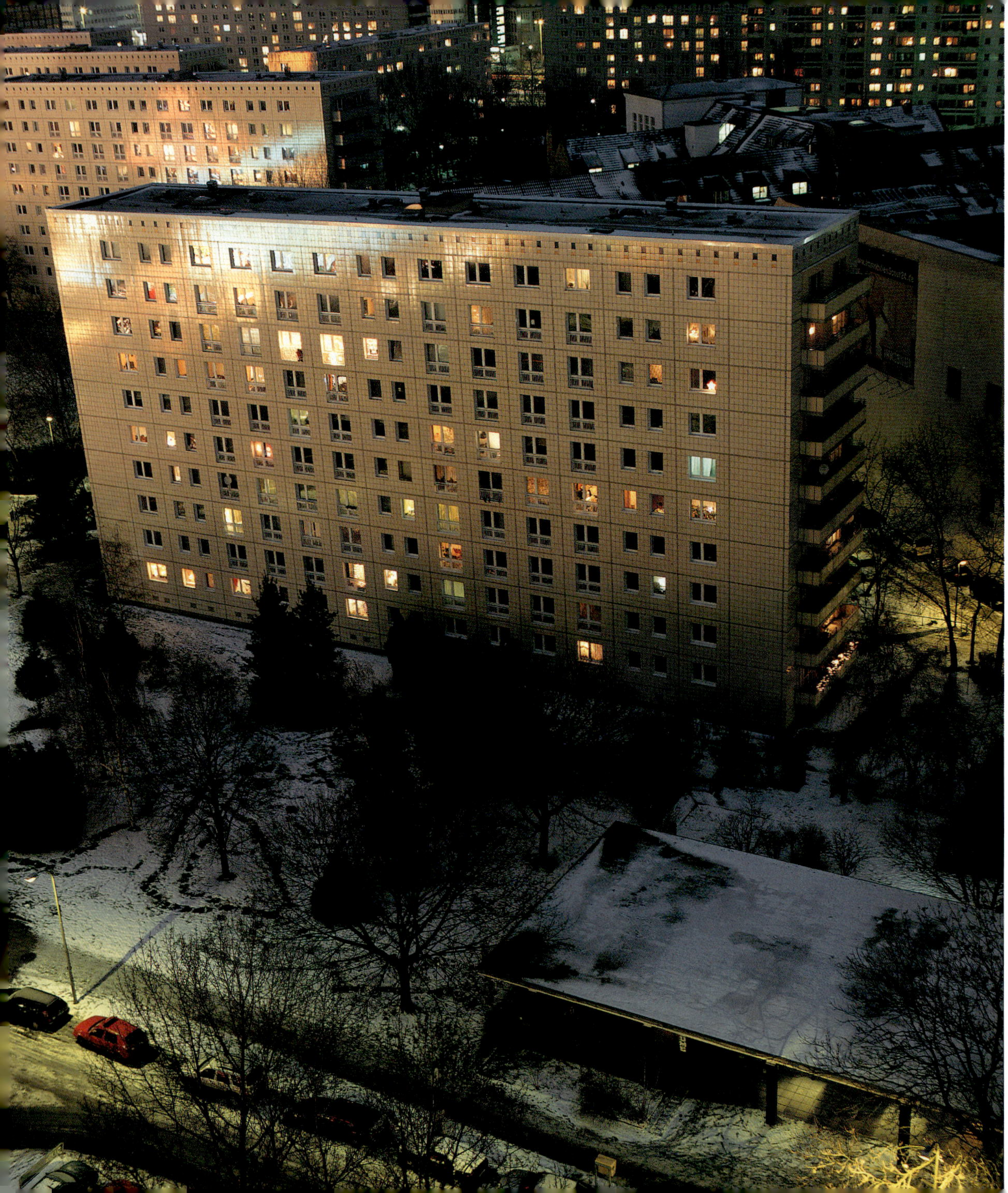

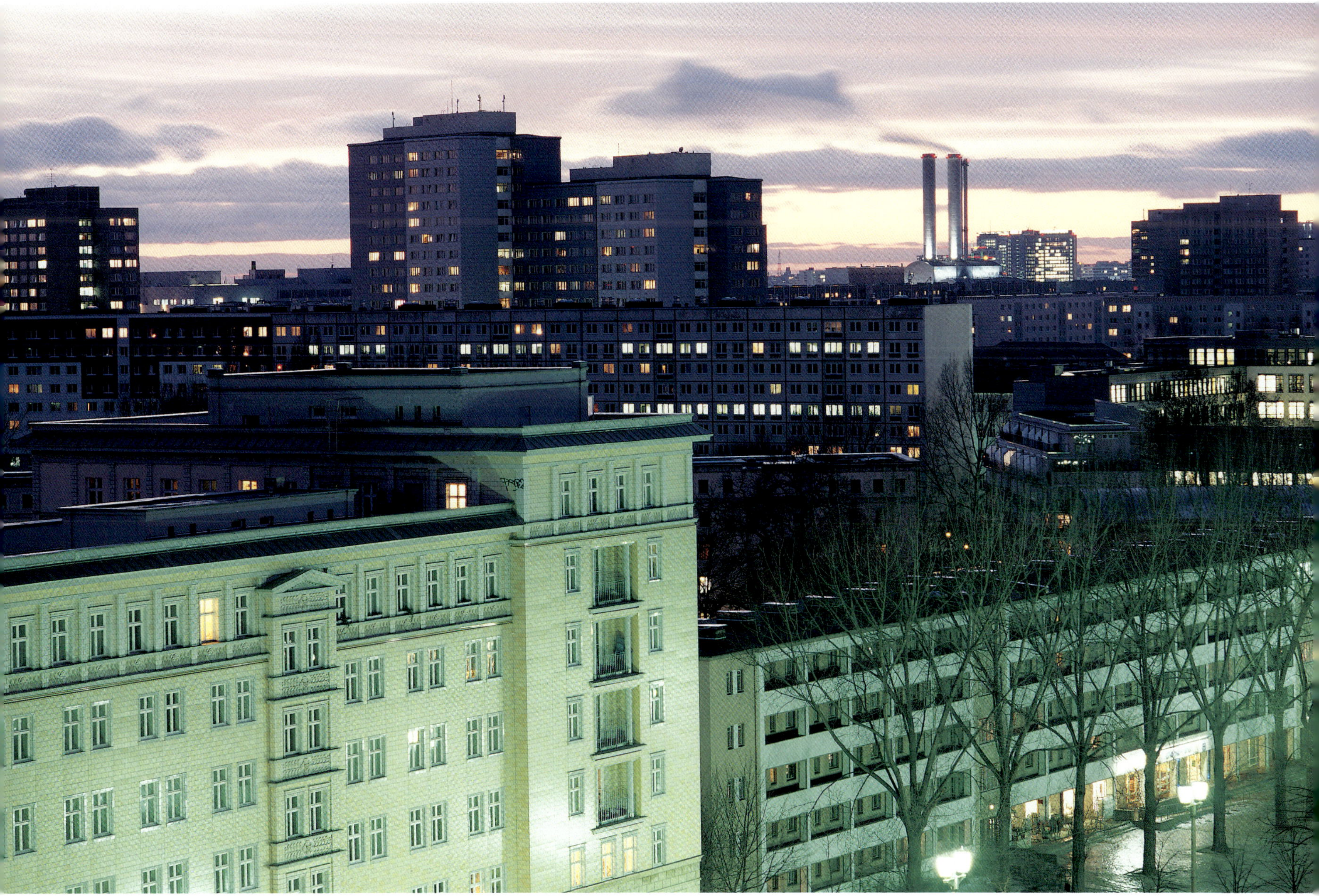

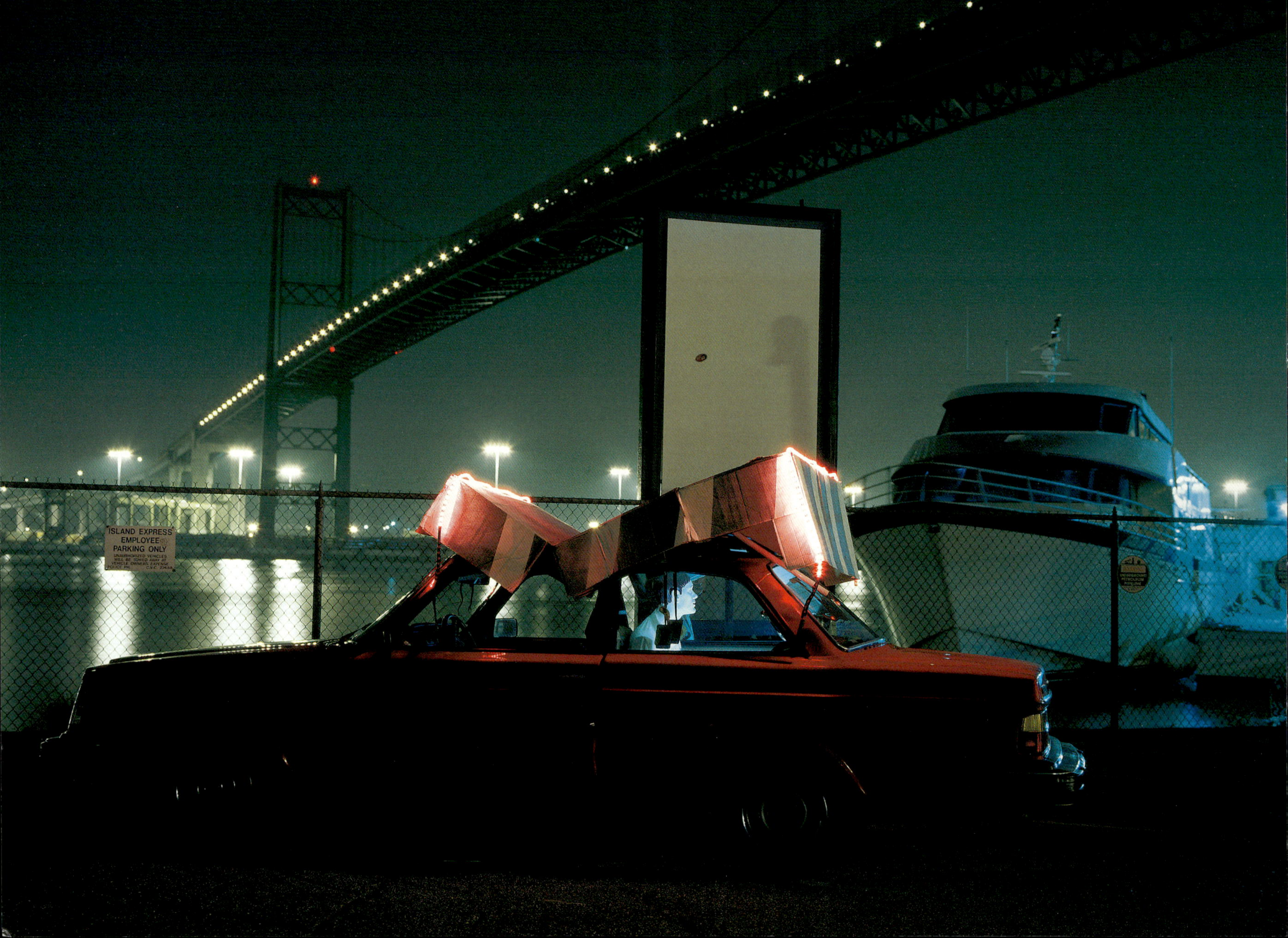
ISLAND EXPRESS
EMPLOYEE
PARKING ONLY

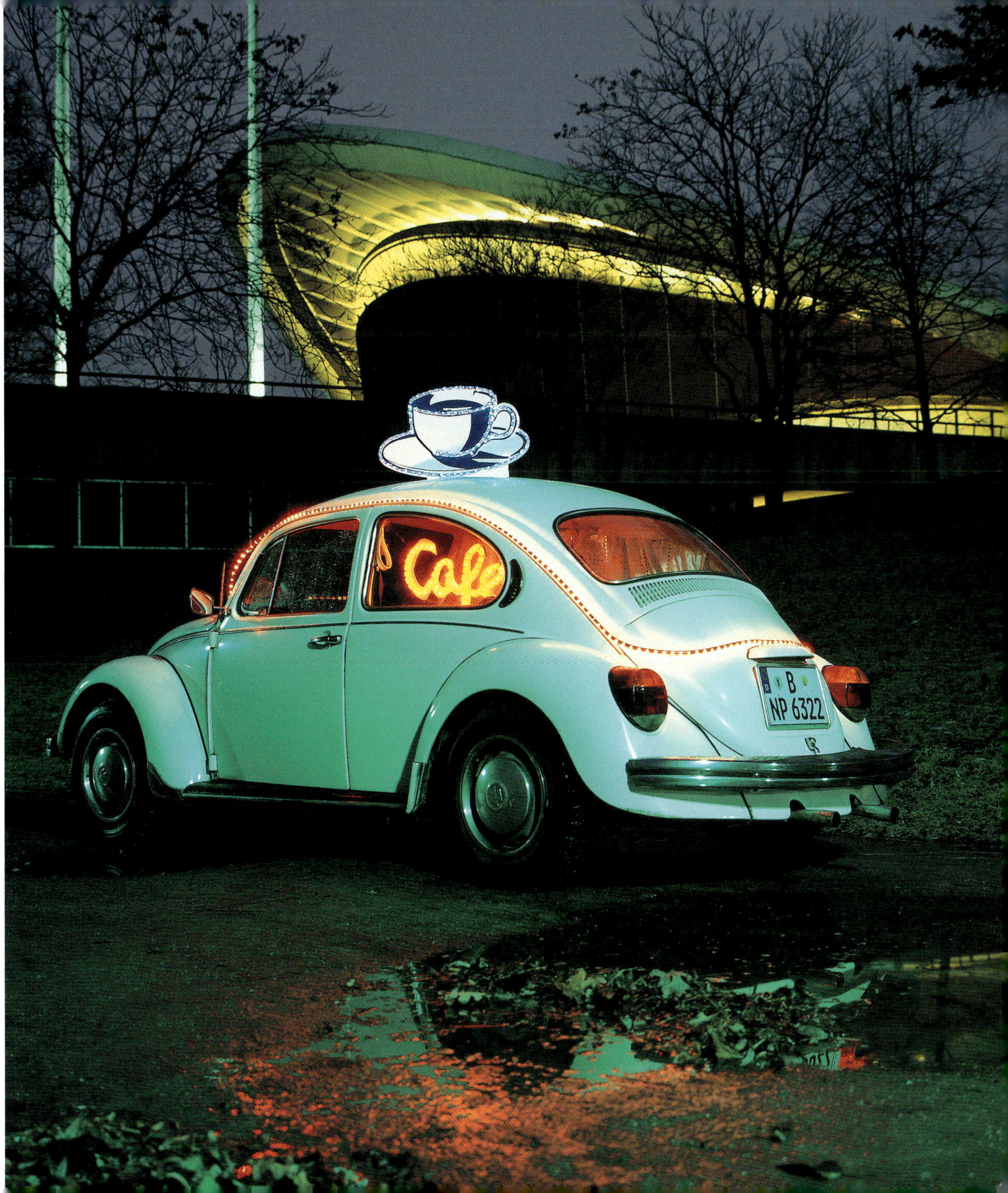
Cafe
B
NP 6322

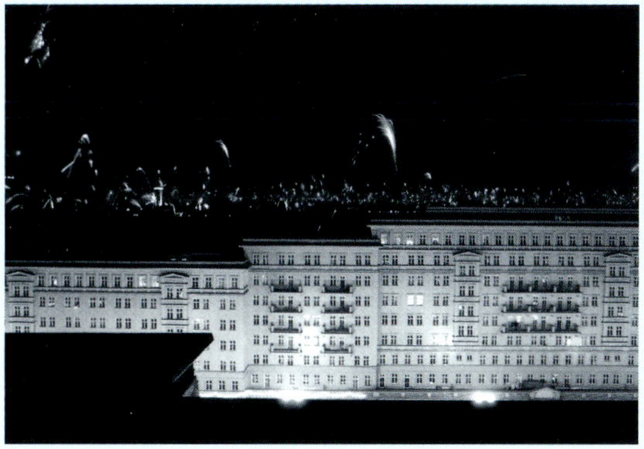

Karl-Marx-Allee, 01.01.02

Oliver Elser

Gespensterbilder – Ghost Pictures

Das elektrische Licht, die Fotografie und die Architektur der Moderne sind Geschwister, Kinder derselben Zeit. Nimmt man noch das einige Jahrzehnte jüngere Automobil dazu, dann entsteht wie von selbst das Porträt der Großstadt des zwanzigsten Jahrhunderts. Dieser Satz ist wahr, solange ich ihn in Berlin auf meinem Monitor sehe. Jetzt, an einem geborgten Schreibtisch in Wien, klingt er wie eine Beschwörungsformel. Statt *Geschwister* lese ich *Gespenster* und bin überrascht, wie gut das passt, wenn ich mir Eva Castringius' Fotos anschaue. Es sind freundliche Gespenster des zwanzigsten Jahrhunderts darauf zu sehen – die knochenbleichen Fassaden der Berliner Karl-Marx-Allee, das zum Wirtschaftswunderwagen umfrisierte *Kraft-durch-Freude*-Auto, der Familienpanzer aus Schwedenstahl, die handgeformten Neonzeichen der industrialisierten Diner-Restaurantbetriebe. Auch hier in Wien konnte man in den sechziger Jahren eine Dia-Serie kaufen, die die Stadt bei Nacht zeigte, nur war es die alte Stadt, historische Baudenkmäler in Natriumdampflampenlicht, das überall dieselbe Atmosphäre schafft, weil es „das [Farb-] Spektrum verfickt", wie die Nachkriegs-Jugendlichen in Julian Barnes' *Metroland* enttäuscht feststellen. Die Neon-Szenen in Los Angeles und Berlin hingegen sind Momentaufnahmen einer anderen Realität, in ihnen erfährt die Moderne ihre *blaue Stunde*. Licht, Himmel und Architektur entfachen einen Postkartenzauber, in dessen utopischer Welt die Zukunftsversprechen der abgebildeten Bauten noch einmal aufleuchten dürfen.

Electric light, photography and modern architecture are siblings, children of the same age. If one adds the car, which is a few decades younger, the portrait of the twentieth-century city emerges as if from nowhere. This sentence is true as long as I see it on my computer-screen in Berlin. Now, sitting at a borrowed desk in Vienna, it sounds like an incantation. In place of *siblings* I read *spirits* and am surprised at how fitting this is when I look at Eva Castringius' photos. In these photos, one can see friendly spirits or rather ghosts of the twentieth century – the pale bone-colored façades of Berlin's Karl-Marx-Allee, the *Kraft-durch-Freude* car that has become a symbol of the economic miracle, the family tank made of Swedish steel, the hand-made neon signs welcoming you to the industrialized diner restaurants. Here, in Vienna in the Sixties one could also purchase a slide series showing the city at night, but it was the old city – historical monuments in artificial gas lighting – that created the same atmosphere everywhere, because it "fucks-up the color spectrum" as the post-war youth in Julian Barnes' *Metroland* disappointedly ascertains. On the other hand, the neon scenes in Los Angeles and Berlin are frozen moments of another reality, one where the modern age experiences its *blue hour*. Light, sky and architecture produce a post-card magic, in whose utopian world the buildings' promises for the future are allowed to light up once more.

Nicola Kuhn

From Dusk Till Dawn

Der Himmel über Berlin und der Horizont von Los Angeles – beide haben Berühmtheit erlangt, in der Kunst, in der Literatur, im Film. Sie sind ein Sehnsuchtsmotiv, ein Gegenüber für den Moloch Großstadt. Eva Castringius hat in ihrer Fotoserie *The Big Sky* die Horizontlinie von Europa nach Amerika weitergezogen, die luftigen Sphären beider Städte zusammengespannt. Herausgekommen ist keine romantische Ballade, keine schwermütige Abhandlung oder nüchterne Metropolenfotografie, sondern eine sehr persönliche Reise durch zwei Städte mit einem ebenso ungewöhnlichen wie nahe liegendem Vehikel: dem Wagen der Künstlerin. Ein Automobil ist beiderseits des Atlantiks Protagonist, nicht nur Requisite dieser Fotogeschichten, die ihren Ausgang in Los Angeles genommen haben. Dort hatte die Berliner Künstlerin im Sommer 2001 in der Villa Aurora ein Stipendium absolviert und die erste Serie fotografiert, die sich nun mit Bildern ihrer Heimatstadt zu einer neuen Erzählung mischt.

Eva Castringius schildert Geschichten der etwas anderen Art: kein Fotoroman, sondern Anhaltspunkte eines Geschehens, das sich der Betrachter selbst rekonstruieren muss. Hauptdarstellerin ist die Stadt selbst. Das immer wiederkehrende Motiv des Autos – in Los Angeles der rote Volvo, in Berlin der weiße VW-Käfer – dient vor allem als Bindeglied. Beide Fahrzeuge hat die Künstlerin mit einfachsten Mitteln neu gestaltet und damit zu mobilen Repräsentanten einer festen Lokalität gemacht. Der hinzugefügte Dachaufbau des Volvos greift die Silhouette von *Johnie's Restaurant* auf, einem berühmten Fünfziger-Jahre-Diner inmitten der Miracle Mile von Los Angeles, der heute nur noch als nostalgische Filmkulisse dient, bis Bodenspekulanten in naher Zukunft selbst dieser Funktion ein Ende bereiten werden. Den VW-Käfer hingegen ziert als Symbol eine Tasse. Beide Fahrzeuge werden durch Lichterketten konturiert und mit dem schwungvollen Schriftzug *Johnie's Restaurant* und *Café* zusätzlich erleuchtet.

Mittels dieser beiden Fahrzeuge bringt Eva Castringius das urbane Umfeld neu zum Klingen. Als Resonanzkörper städtischen Lebens sind sie eine künstlerische Invention: durch ihre eigenartige Zwitterrolle, in die sie durch die Zusatzarrangements schlüpfen, beginnt sich das Stadtbild um sie herum neu zu orientieren. Die Szenen zeigen bekannte und berühmte Schauplätze, auf die man nun eine andere Sicht gewinnt. Es sind der Hafen von

Long Beach, der LAX-Airport oder der Pacific Coast Highway in Los Angeles; das Internationale Congress Centrum (ICC), das Haus der Kulturen der Welt oder der Bierpinsel in Berlin. Während Eva Castringius im sommerlichen Los Angeles vornehmlich in der Abenddämmerung fotografierte und dadurch das Gespenstische dieses vagabundierenden Diners erhöhte, machte sie einen großen Teil ihrer Berliner Aufnahmen im Morgengrauen. Die besondere Färbung des Morgenhimmels verleiht den Bildern sphärisches Licht und lässt die gezeigten Gebäude wie Raumschiffe erscheinen.

Eva Castringius zeigt inszenierte Blicke, keineswegs Stadtporträts. Die von ihr ausgewählten Standorte verbindet jedoch alle eine bestimmte Historizität, die noch einmal durch die nostalgischen Schriftzüge ihrer rollenden Protagonisten unterstrichen wird. *Johnie's Restaurant* ist ein typischer Vertreter jener schnell in den fünfziger Jahren aus dem Boden gestampften Googie-Architektur, die im Zuge des damaligen Baubooms entstand und sich durch besondere Material- und Formenkombinationen sowie ausladende Neonbeleuchtungen auszeichnet. Dieser zeitliche Bezug kehrt auch in den Berlin-Bildern wieder, etwa in der 1958 von Hugh Stubbins erbauten Kongresshalle, dem heutigen Haus der Kulturen der Welt, das im Rahmen der Internationalen Bauausstellung als Geschenk des amerikanischen Volkes an West-Berlin gebaut wurde. Als Pendant im Osten zeigt Eva Castringius einen Blick auf Hermann Henselmanns zeitgleich entstandene Karl-Marx-Allee sowie die Kongresshalle unweit vom Alexanderplatz, deren Kuppel sich ebenso wie das geschwungene Dach des Stubbins-Baus in den Rundungen des VW-Käfers reflektiert.

In diesen Bildern ist der urbane Raum Projektionsfläche der Fantasie, die zusätzlich animiert wird durch die eigens gestalteten Fahrzeuge sowie die besonderen Lichtreflexe im Dunkeln. *The Big Sky* meint die Weite des Horizonts, der all dies überspannt. In Eva Castringius' Fotografien finden die Geschichten darunter ihre Erfüllung: die in den Himmel gelenkte Sehnsucht, die Suche nach dem Anderen in der Stadt findet ihre Erwiderung in den Straßen und Gebäuden selbst.

The sky over Berlin and Los Angeles' horizon – both have become famous, in art, literature and film. They are motifs of longing, counterparts of the urban swamp. In her photo series *The Big Sky*, Eva Castringius has extended the line of the horizon from Europe to America, bringing the airy spheres of both cities together. The result is not a romantic ballad, a weighty discourse or mere sober urban photography, but a very personal journey through two cities in an unusual yet obvious vehicle: the artist's car. On both sides of the Atlantic an automobile is the protagonist and not just a prop in these two photo stories that started in Los Angeles. L.A. is where the Berlin artist spent the summer of 2001, on a grant at the Villa Aurora. It is also where she photographed the first series that she has now complemented with photographs of her native city.

Eva Castringius tells slightly different stories: the viewer is not presented with an epic photo story but with certain hints that the observer needs to piece together for himself. The city itself is the main actor. The car as the ever-recurring motif – in Los Angeles the red Volvo, in Berlin the white Volkswagen Beetle – above all serves as a connecting link. The artist used simple means to refashion both cars, thereby making them into mobile representatives of a fixed locality. The VW Beetle is crowned with a symbolic cup and the Volvo's added roof piece is a reference to the silhouette of *Johnie's Restaurant*, a famous Fifties diner at the heart of Los Angeles's Miracle Mile. Today, the diner only serves as a nostalgic setting for films. In the near future, though, land speculation is sure to put an end to even this function. Both vehicles are outlined with strings of lights and are, moreover, illuminated by a flourish of lettering reading *Johnie's Restaurant* and *Café* respectively.

Through these two cars, Eva Castringius makes the urban environment vibrate in a new way. As a soundbox for urban life they are an artistic invention: through their strange hybrid role, the cityscape begins to re-orient itself around them. The scenes show well-known locations, and so one gains a new perspective on: the Long Beach Docks, LAX Airport or the Pacific Coast Highway in Los Angeles; the Internationales Congress Centrum (ICC), the

Haus der Kulturen der Welt or the restaurant called Bierpinsel in Berlin. While in sunny Los Angeles the artist primarily photographed at dusk, thereby increasing the eeriness of this vagrant diner, she took a large part of the Berlin pictures at dawn. The particular tinge of the morning sky fills the photos with celestial light making the buildings look like spaceships.

Eva Castringius shows constructed views and by no means city portraits. However, a certain historicizing notion links all the locations she selects. And this notion is enhanced by the nostalgic words decorating her motorized protagonists. *Johnie's Restaurant* is a restaurant from the Fifties. It is a typical representative of the Googie architecture that sprung up overnight in the course of a building rush. A particular fusion of material and form as well as elaborate neon lighting characterize this type of architecture. This temporal reference also appears in the Berlin pictures, in the Kongresshalle built in 1958 by Hugh Stubbins, and in today's Haus der Kulturen der Welt that came into being in the context of the International Building Exhibition as a present from the American people to West Berlin. As its Eastern counterpart, Eva Castringius presents a view of Hermann Henselmann's Karl-Marx-Allee that was built around the same time. She also presents an image of the other Congress Hall not far from Alexanderplatz. The Congress Hall's dome as well as the curved roof of Stubbins' building are mirrored in the VW Beetle's curves.

In these pictures, the urban space becomes a projection surface for the imagination, which the uniquely fashioned vehicles stimulate further as do the special light reflections at night. *The Big Sky* refers to the breadth of the horizon spanning it all. In Eva Castringius' photographs, the stories find their fulfillment under this sky: longing directed up into the sky and the search for otherness in the city find their reply in the streets and buildings themselves.

Abbildungen – Plates

Johnie's Restaurant
Los Angeles, 2001
89 x 111 cm

Märkisches Viertel I
Berlin, 2002
89 x 111 cm

Pacific Palisades
Los Angeles, 2001
74 x 111 cm

Hollywood
Los Angeles, 2001
74 x 111 cm

Gropiusstadt I
Berlin, 2002
89 x 111 cm

Gropiusstadt II
Berlin, 2002
89 x 111 cm

Hollywood Hills
Los Angeles, 2001
74 x 111 cm

Chinatown
Los Angeles, 2001
74 x 111 cm

Avus
Berlin, 2002
89 x 111 cm

Märkisches Viertel II
Berlin, 2002
89 x 111 cm

Hi Life
Los Angeles, 2001
111 x 74 cm

LAX Airport I
Los Angeles, 2001
89 x 111 cm

Kongresshalle
Berlin, 2002
89 x 111 cm

Alexanderstraße
Berlin, 2002
111 x 89 cm

City Walk
Los Angeles, 2001
74 x 111 cm

Pacific Cost Highway
Los Angeles, 2001
89 x 111 cm

International Congress Center
Los Angeles, 2001
111 x 89 cm

Christiansen Kugel
Los Angeles, 2001
111 x 89 cm

Gas station
Los Angeles, 2001
89 x 111 cm

Everett Place
Los Angeles, 2001
89 x 111 cm

Mackey Apartments
Los Angeles, 2001
74 x 111 cm

Todeshochhaus
Berlin, 2002
89 x 111 cm

LAX Airport II
Los Angeles, 2001
89 x 111 cm

South Central
Los Angeles, 2001
111 x 89 cm

Bierpinsel
Berlin, 2002
111 x 89 cm

Wohnblock Mitte
Berlin, 2002
111 x 89 cm

Karl-Marx-Allee
Berlin, 2002
89 x 111 cm

Williamsbridge
Los Angeles, 2001
89 x 111 cm

Haus der Kulturen der Welt
Berlin, 2002
111 x 89 cm

alle Arbeiten: Ilfochrome auf Al-Dibond
all works: Ilfochrome on Al-Dibond

Eva Castringius

1967 geboren in München
born in Munich

1993–99 Studium der Malerei und Fotografie an der Hochschule der Künste, Berlin; Meisterschülerabschluss
studied painting and photography at the Hochschule der Künste, Berlin

1996 Erasmusstipendium im Royal College of Art, London
scholarship for the Royal College of Art, London

1999 Karl-Hofer Stipendium, Berlin
Karl Hofer scholarship, Berlin

2001 Stipendium der Villa Aurora, Los Angeles
Villa Aurora scholarship, Los Angeles

2001 Atelierpreis der Karl-Hofer-Gesellschaft, Berlin
studio prize from the Karl Hofer Gesellschaft, Berlin

Einzelausstellungen
Solo Exhibitions

2002 *The Big Sky – Los Angeles-Berlin*, Martin-Gropius-Bau, Berlin
2001 *The Big Sky*, pepperprojects, Berlin
2000 *supera galactica*, Galerie Martin Kudlek, Köln
1999 *superworld*, Galerie Kunstruimte, Berlin
underground, Galerie dirty windows, Berlin

Gruppenausstellungen
Group Exhibitions

2001 *Johnie's Restaurant*, Three Day Weekend Gallery, Los Angeles
2000 *Zeichnungen*, Galerie Martin Kudlek, Köln
1999 *untold stories*, Galerie DeChiara/Stewart, New York
Kleine Welten, Kunst- und Medienzentrum Adlershof, Berlin
Foto, Galerie Edda Biermann/dirty windows, Berlin
1997 *Rotterdam–Berlin*, Galerie De Brieder, Rotterdam

Dank – Acknowledgements

Villa Aurora e.V.
Dr. Mechthild Borries-Knopp, Dr. Joachim Bernauer, Freimut Duve, Claudia Gordon

Neuer Berliner Kunstverein
Dr. Alexander Tolnay

Karl-Hofer-Gesellschaft
Jürgen Schleicher, Erwin Staudt, Matthias Langner, Utha Herzbruch-Rueß

Berliner Festspiele
Gereon Sievernich, Katrin Mundorf

photomarketing.de
Dr. Bernd Fechner

Galerien – Galleries:
pepperprojects, Jens Pepper
Galerie Martin Kudlek

Hyp Berlin
Detlef Untermann, Nicole Hanke

CCS – Fachlabor für Farbfotografie
Hans Ruh, Halina Makarewizc, Andreas Latuska

Nicola Kuhn, Oliver Elser,
Stephan Fiedler, Thorsten Platz

Impressum – Imprint

Diese Publikation erscheint anlässlich der Ausstellung *Eva Castringius – The Big Sky* im Martin-Gropius-Bau, Berlin, veranstaltet durch die Villa Aurora e.V. in Zusammenarbeit mit dem Neuen Berliner Kunstverein und der Karl-Hofer-Gesellschaft.

This publication is issued on the occasion of the exhibition *Eva Castringius – The Big Sky* at the Martin Gropius Bau, Berlin, commissioned jointly by the Villa Aurora e.V. in cooperation with the Neuer Berliner Kunstverein and the Karl Hofer Gesellschaft.

Zitat / Quotation Jean Baudrillard:
Amerika, München, Matthes & Seitz Verlag, 1995, S.76–77
America, London/New York, Verso Books, 1989, pp. 52–53

Mit freundlicher Unterstützung von
With the friendly support of

VOLVO

Konzept / Concept:
Eva Castringius

Autoren / Authors:
Nicola Kuhn, Oliver Elser

Übersetzung / Translation:
Martin Kudlek

Gestaltung / Design:
Stephan Fiedler

Lithografie / Lithography:
Licht & Tiefe, Berlin

Druck / Printing:
Druckerei Heenemann, Berlin

Jovis Verlag GmbH
Kurfürstenstraße 15/16
D-10785 Berlin

ISBN 3-931321-28-2